T0001936

Best Easy Day Hikes
Mount Rainier National Park

Help Us Keep This Guide Up to Date

Every effort has been made by the authors and editors to make this guide as accurate and useful as possible. However, many things can change after a guide is published—regulations change, facilities come under new management, and so forth.

We would love to hear from you concerning your experiences with this guide and how you feel it could be improved and kept up to date. While we may not be able to respond to all comments and suggestions, we'll take them to heart, and we'll also make certain to share them with the authors. Please send your comments and suggestions to falconeditorial@rowman.com.

Thanks for your input!

Best Easy Day Hikes Series

Best Easy Day Hikes Mount Rainier National Park

Fifth Edition

Mary Skjelset and Heidi Radlinski

FALCONGUIDES

ESSEX, CONNECTICUT

FALCONGUIDES®

An imprint of Globe Pequot, the trade division of
The Rowman & Littlefield Publishing Group, Inc.
4501 Forbes Blvd., Ste. 200
Lanham, MD 20706
www.rowman.com

Distributed by NATIONAL BOOK NETWORK

British Library Cataloguing-in-Publication Information Available

Library of Congress Cataloging-in-Publication Data Available

ISBN 978-1-4930-7755-7 (paper: alk. paper)
ISBN 978-1-4930-7754-0 (electronic)

♾™ The paper used in this publication meets the minimum requirements of American National Standard for Information Sciences—Permanence of Paper for Printed Library Materials, ANSI/NISO Z39.48-1992.

Contents

The Hikes

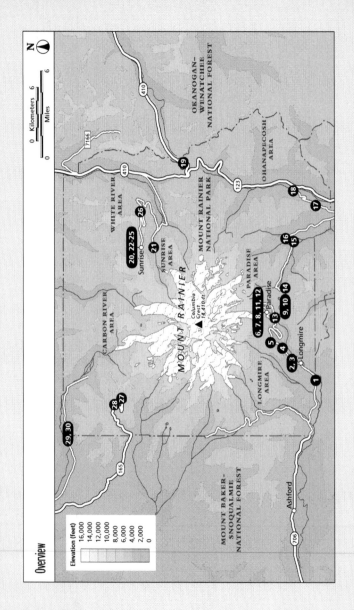

Overview

Elevation (feet)
16,000
14,000
12,000
10,000
8,000
6,000
4,000
2,000
0

MOUNT BAKER-
SNOQUALMIE
NATIONAL FOREST

CARBON RIVER
AREA

WHITE RIVER
AREA

OKANOGAN-
WENATCHEE
NATIONAL FOREST

MOUNT RAINIER
NATIONAL PARK

SUNRISE
AREA

Sunrise

OHANAPECOSH
AREA

Columbia
Crest
14,410 ft.

PARADISE
AREA

Paradise

LONGMIRE
AREA

Longmire

Ashford

N

0 Kilometers 6
0 Miles 6

What Is a "Best Easy Day Hike"?

Best Easy Day Hikes Mount Rainier National Park includes shorter, less-strenuous hikes that we recommend for nice, casual day hikes in Mount Rainier National Park.

The thirty hikes in this book are located in all four quadrants of Mount Rainier National Park. All hikes in this guide are on easy-to-follow trails with no off-trail sections. The trailheads—for the most part—are easy to access and require only a two-wheel-drive vehicle. A trail map and detailed driving instructions help you reach the trailhead and orient yourself once there.

These hikes vary in length from 0.3 to 6.4 miles. Most range between 1 and 5 miles total. Some of the hikes in this book might not seem easy to some hikers. The geography of Mount Rainier does not lend itself to very easy hikes. Steep glaciated valleys and volcanic ridges dominate the landscape. Unparalleled scenery, however, rewards the hiker willing to put in the extra effort.

That said, we have made certain that this guide has a hike for everyone. To help you decide, we have ranked the hikes from easiest to hardest. Please keep in mind that short does not always equal easy. Other factors such as elevation gain and trail conditions must be considered.

We hope you thoroughly enjoy your best "easy" hiking experiences in Mount Rainier National Park.

— Mary Skjelset and Heidi Radlinski

Planning Your Trip

Timed Entry Reservations

In 2024, the National Park Service initiated a pilot program for timed entry reservations. Dramatic increases in visitation had resulted in overcrowding and congestion in parking lots, visitor facilities, and on the trails. The two most popular corridors—Paradise and Sunrise—now require a timed reservation between 7 a.m. and 3 p.m. in the summer months. While this may resolve some of the delays noted in the hike descriptions, it does require additional planning. Visit the Park website for more information about the entrance stations affected or to reserve your spot in the queue: www.nps .gov/mora/planyourvisit/timed-entry-reservations.htm.

Wilderness Information Centers

Longmire Wilderness Information Center: (360) 569-6650

Open late May to October, the Longmire Wilderness Information Center issues wilderness camping permits primarily for backpacking. The center has rangers equipped to help with any questions you might have, as well as a large relief map of the park. The Longmire Wilderness Information Center is located in the Longmire Historic District, along Longmire-Paradise Road. From the Nisqually Entrance Station, drive 6.7 miles east to the Longmire Historic District.

Paradise Guide House (Climbing Information Center): (360) 569-6641

The Paradise Guide House mainly issues climbing permits for routes starting from Paradise, but you can obtain wilderness camping permits and other information here as well. This ranger station is open mid-May through summer. From the Nisqually Entrance Station, drive 15.9 miles east on Longmire-Paradise Road to the intersection with Stevens Canyon Road. Stay to the left and head 2.2 miles up to the Paradise Complex. From the Stevens Canyon Entrance Station, drive nearly 19 miles west on the Stevens Canyon Road to the intersection with the Longmire-Paradise Road. Turn right (north) and follow the signs to Paradise.

White River Wilderness Information Center: (360) 569-6670

This center issues permits primarily for backpacking and north-side climbing routes. Open late May through mid-October, the White River Wilderness Information Center is located next to the White River Entrance Station.

Carbon River Ranger Station: (360) 829-9639

Located 2 miles west of the Carbon River Entrance, the Carbon River Ranger Station issues permits in the Carbon River region and provides other information about the area. The station is staffed year-round, but its hours of operation expand during the summer, particularly on weekends. Call in advance for specific information. From Wilkeson, continue for 9 miles along WA 165 to where the road forks, go to the left (east) onto Carbon River Road. In 6 miles, you will see the station on your left (north).

Visitor Centers and Museums

Longmire Museum: (360) 569-6575

Open year-round, the Longmire Museum offers a range of information, such as natural history, cultural history, backpacking, hiking, and trail conditions. It also issues permits when the Longmire Wilderness Information Center is closed. The Longmire Museum is located in the Longmire Historic District, along Longmire-Paradise Road. From the Nisqually Entrance Station, drive 6.7 miles east to the Longmire Historic District.

Henry M. Jackson Memorial Visitor Center at Paradise: (360) 569-6571

The Henry M. Jackson Memorial Visitor Center is located in the Paradise Complex and offers a variety of natural and cultural information through exhibits, films, guided walks, and nature talks. Reconstructed in 2008 to meet energy efficiency and accessibility standards, the visitor center also houses a snack bar, gift shop, and public restroom. The park staff also issues wilderness permits. The visitor center is open year-round (weekends and holidays only from early October to mid-May). From the Nisqually Entrance Station, drive 15.9 miles east on Longmire-Paradise Road to the intersection with Stevens Canyon Road. Stay to the left and head 2.2 miles up to the Paradise Complex. From the Stevens Canyon Entrance Station, drive nearly 19 miles west on the Stevens Canyon Road to the intersection with the Longmire-Paradise Road. Turn right (north) and follow the signs to Paradise.

Sunrise Visitor Center: (360) 663-2425

The Sunrise Visitor Center provides a wealth of historical and geological information about Mount Rainier National

Park. It generally opens in early July, about the time the White River Road opens, and closes in mid-September. From the White River Entrance Station, drive 13.8 miles west on White River Road to the Sunrise Complex.

Ohanapecosh Visitor Center: (360) 569-6581
The Ohanapecosh Visitor Center provides a variety of exhibits and information about Mount Rainier National Park at the entrance to Ohanapecosh Campground. The visitor center usually opens after Memorial Day and stays open through Columbus Day weekend in October. From the Stevens Canyon Entrance Station, drive 1.8 miles south on WA 123 to the turnoff for Ohanapecosh Campground. The road forks just after you turn in; go right (north) and drive until the Ohanapecosh Visitor Center appears directly in front of you.

Website and Social Media

Mount Rainier National Park website: www.nps .gov/mora/planyourvisit/index.htm
The park website has a plethora of relevant, timely information about the park. We recommend checking the website while you are planning your trip. It is also helpful right before you go to get information on current trail conditions, road closures, and other important updates.

www.facebook.com/MountRainierNPS, www .instagram.com/mountrainiernps/
The Park also hosts official Facebook and Instagram pages with news, updates, fun facts, in-depth articles, and photographs.

Leave No Trace

Going into a national park such as Mount Rainier is like visiting a museum. You obviously do not want to leave your mark on an art treasure in the museum. If everybody going through the museum left one little mark, the piece of art would be quickly destroyed—and of what value is a big building full of trashed art? The same goes for a pristine wilderness such as Mount Rainier National Park, which is as magnificent as any masterpiece made by human hands. If we all left just one little mark on the landscape, the wilderness would soon be despoiled.

A wilderness can accommodate human use as long as everybody behaves, but a few thoughtless or uninformed visitors can ruin it for everybody who follows. All wilderness users have a responsibility to know and follow the rules of Leave No Trace camping.

Nowadays most wilderness users want to walk softly, but some are not aware that they have poor manners. Often their actions are dictated by the outdated habits of a past generation of campers, who cut green boughs for evening shelters, built campfires with fire rings, and dug trenches around tents. These outdated camping modes may have been acceptable in the 1950s, but they leave long-lasting scars. Today such behavior is absolutely unacceptable. The wilderness is shrinking, and the number of users is mushrooming. More and more camping areas show unsightly signs of heavy use.

A new code of ethics has grown out of the necessity of coping with the unending waves of people who want an enjoyable wilderness experience. Today we all must leave no clues that we have gone before. Canoeists can look behind the canoe and see no trace of their passing. Hikers, mountain bikers, and four-wheelers should have the same goal. Enjoy the wildness, but leave no trace on the landscape.

Three Leave No Trace Principles
Leave with everything you brought.
Leave no sign of your visit.
Leave the landscape as you found it.

Most of us know better than to litter—in or out of the wilderness. Be sure you leave no items, regardless of how small, along the trail or at the campsite. Pack out everything, including orange peels, flip tops, cigarette butts, and gum wrappers. Also pick up any trash that others have left behind.

Follow the main trail. Avoid cutting switchbacks and walking on vegetation beside the trail.

Do not pick up "souvenirs," such as rocks, antlers, or wildflowers. The next person wants to see them too, and taking such items with you violates park regulations.

Avoid making loud noises that may disturb others. Remember, sound travels easily to the other side of lakes. Be courteous.

Carry a lightweight trowel to bury human waste 6 to 8 inches deep, and pack out used toilet paper. Keep human waste at least 300 feet from any water source.

Finally, and perhaps most important, strictly follow the pack-in/pack-out rule. If you carry something into the back-country, consume it or carry it out.

Practice Leave No Trace principles—and put your ear to the ground in the wilderness and listen carefully. Thousands of people coming behind you are thanking you for your courtesy and good sense.

For more information and helpful tips, visit © Leave No Trace: www.LNT.org.

A Note on Your Furry Friends

If you love hiking with your loyal companion, Mount Rainier is not your ideal destination. To preserve wildlife, the National Park Service prohibits pets on trails, in the wilderness and/or off-trail areas, inside buildings, in amphitheaters and on snow-covered roads closed for winter (except designated snowmobile routes). Therefore, the vast majority of trails and land in the park remains off-limits to your furry friend. There are a few, narrow exceptions:

Pacific Crest Trail—Dogs are permitted on the Pacific Crest Trail (PCT). They must be on a leash no longer than 6 feet. Of the best easy day hikes in this book, only Hike 19: Naches Peak has a portion of the trail outside the park or along the PCT.

Designated snowmobile routes—In winter, you may bring a dog along the designated snowmobile routes once the following roads are covered with snow: Road to Round Pass, Cougar Rock Campground Loops, WA 123 to Stevens Canyon Road as far as Box Canyon, and WA 410 from the north boundary to White River Road as far as the White River Campground.

Service animals—A service dog is allowed on trails and facilities if the dog has been trained to do work or perform tasks for the benefit of an individual with a disability. This does not include "therapy animals" that provide emotional support.

Pets are permitted in parking lots, campgrounds, and on paved roads. However, at all times they must be leashed or crated and with their owners.

For more information, visit https://www.nps.gov/mora/planyourvisit/pets.htm.

Ranking the Hikes

The following list ranks the hikes in this book from easiest to hardest.

13.	Narada Falls
30.	Carbon River Rainforest Trail
16.	Box Canyon
3.	Trail of the Shadows
1.	Twin Firs Loop
20.	Silver Forest
18.	Grove of the Patriarchs
7.	Nisqually Vista
29.	Old Mine Trail
25.	Sourdough Ridge Nature Trail
6.	Alta Vista Summit
8.	Dead Horse Creek
17.	Silver Falls
21.	Emmons Moraine
9.	High Lakes Trail
15.	Stevens Creek
4.	Carter Falls
14.	Snow Lake
27.	Spray Falls
26.	Dege Peak
19.	Naches Peak
10.	Pinnacle Peak Saddle
22.	Mount Fremont Lookout
24.	Sunrise Rim
23.	Forest Lake
11.	Paradise Glacier
28.	Tolmie Peak

Map Legend

Symbol	Description	Symbol	Description
12	US Highway	Bridge	Bridge
706	State Highway	▲	Campground
7166	Forest Road	▲	Campsite (back country)
	Local Road	▲	Mountain/Peak
	Unimproved Road	P	Parking
	Featured Trail	Pass/Gap	Pass/Gap
	Trail	Picnic Area	Picnic Area
	Back Country Trail	■	Point of Interest/Structure
	Paved Trail	Ranger Station/Guide House	Ranger Station/Guide House
	River/Creek	o	Town
	Intermittent Stream	Trailhead	Trailhead
	Body of Water	Tunnel	Tunnel
	Glacier	Viewpoint/Overlook	Viewpoint/Overlook
	Marsh	Visitor/Information Center	Visitor/Information Center
	National Forest	Waterfall	Waterfall

1 Twin Firs Loop

This short loop circles a low-elevation old-growth forest dominated by western red cedar and Douglas fir that reach for the sky, and vine maple, skunk cabbage, and giant ferns that carpet the forest floor.

Start: Twin Firs Loop Trailhead
Distance: 0.4-mile loop
Hiking time: 20 minutes
Trail surface: Well-maintained; forest floor
Elevation gain: Minimal
Best season: May through Oct
Nearest town: Ashford

Fees and permits: Vehicle or individual entry fee (7 days); annual entry available; timed entry applies
Trail contacts: Longmire Wilderness Information Center, (360) 569-6650

Finding the trailhead: From the Nisqually Entrance Station, drive east for 4.5 miles on the Longmire-Paradise Road. You will see a turnout on the left of the road. If you reach the Longmire Historic District, you have gone too far. **GPS:** N46 44.012' / W121 50.296'

The Hike

An easy and educational stroll through low-elevation forest, the Twin Firs Loop sees many tourists who stop for a brief walk before reaching the Longmire Historic District. The trail is especially popular with families, since even the littlest visitors can hike the entire length and feel triumphant at the end.

At the trailhead, take the time to read an exhibit describing the flora of low-elevation forests. Through pictures and written description, the exhibit explains how to differentiate Douglas fir, western hemlock, and western red cedar.

Twin Firs Loop

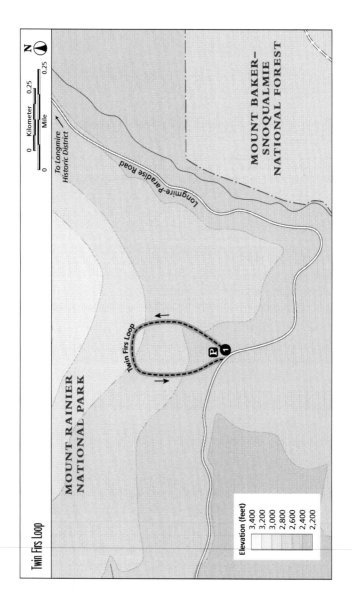

MOUNT RAINIER
NATIONAL PARK

MOUNT BAKER–
SNOQUALMIE
NATIONAL FOREST

To Longmire
Historic District

Longmire-Paradise Road

Twin Firs Loop

P
1

N

0   Kilometer   0.25

0   Mile

Elevation (feet)
3,400
3,200
3,000
2,800
2,600
2,400
2,200

The trail weaves around majestic trees, some fallen and some standing tall. You will see mossy logs and big ferns lining both sides of the trail. Less than halfway into your hike, a log takes you across a small creek to where the trail becomes steeper. You will cross this gurgling creek again just before you return to the Longmire-Paradise Road, directly west of where you began your hike.

Miles and Directions

0.0 Start at the Twin Firs Loop Trailhead.

0.4 Arrive back at Longmire-Paradise Road.

2 Rampart Ridge

One of the few hikes that is clear of snow in June, this short but steep trek up to Rampart Ridge affords peekaboo views of Eagle Peak, Mount Rainier, and the Nisqually River Valley.

Start: Longmire Historic District
Distance: 5.1-mile loop
Hiking time: 2–3 hours
Trail surface: Well-maintained; forest floor
Elevation gain: 1,280 feet
Best season: June through Sept
Nearest town: Ashford

Fees and permits: Vehicle or individual entry fee (7 days); annual entry available; timed entry applies
Trail contacts: Longmire Wilderness Information Center, (360) 569-6650

Finding the trailhead: From Nisqually River Entrance Station, drive 6.7 miles east on the Longmire-Paradise Road to the Longmire Historic District. Turn right (southeast) into the parking lot around the Longmire Historic District, which includes Longmire Wilderness Information Center, the Longmire Museum, and the National Park Inn. Walk on one of the two crosswalks across the Longmire-Paradise Road to the Rampart Ridge Trailhead, located across the street from the inn. **GPS:** N46 45.013' / W121 48.786'

The Hike

This hike is great for people who like to climb hills and need a hike that is snow-free in June. In less than 2 miles, the trail takes you up 1,200 feet and allows you to peer into the valley you just ventured from, as well as the valley on the other side of Rampart Ridge. The ridge itself, also known as the "Ramparts," is a remnant of ancient lava flow from Mount

Rainier. The switchbacks are steep but bearable. Remember to bring plenty of water, because the only water sources arise toward the end of the hike.

We recommend that you hike this trail clockwise to keep possible views of Mount Rainier in front of you. To increase educational opportunities along the hike, we also recommend that you walk the greater part of the Trail of the Shadows. The Trail of the Shadows tells the tale of James Longmire's settlement of the valley where the Longmire Historic District now stands. This tale is told via informational signs posted at points of interest along the way and provides something to think about during your workout ahead.

To start the hike, cross any of the well-marked crosswalks in front of the Longmire Historic District across the Longmire-Paradise Road. Stay to the right (north) until you reach the Trail of the Shadows Trailhead. The Trail of the Shadows (described in detail as Hike 3) is a self-guided hike that loops around a field of mineral springs, past the Longmire cabin, Iron Mike, and the Travertine Mound to the junction with the Rampart Ridge Trail.

At the junction with the Rampart Ridge Trail, go right (north). For more than 1.5 miles there are relatively steep switchbacks, although they level out at the end just before the viewpoints. This part of the trail is mainly in the trees, but at one point you may catch a glimpse of Tumtum Peak to the west. After hiking just over 2 miles, you reach a spur trail that leads to a viewpoint. Take a break and enjoy the scenery from the viewpoint. On a clear day you can see Eagle Peak, the Nisqually River, the Longmire Historic District, and Mount Rainier.

The next 1.2 miles along the ridge are flat and very pleasant. On a clear day, Mount Rainier emerges before you as you cross to the other side of the ridge. On a foggy day, you still have a nice view of the Kautz Creek riverbed in the valley below and Satulick Mountain across the way.

You arrive at the Wonderland Trail junction after traveling a little over a mile from the viewpoint. Go right (south) at this junction. This turn takes you off the Rampart Ridge Trail and onto the Wonderland Trail. From this point on, the trail loses elevation all the way back to the Longmire Historic District. About 0.2 mile after joining the Wonderland Trail, a trail leading to Van Trump Park splits off to the left (northeast). Stay to the right (south) here and continue down the Wonderland Trail. At 4.9 miles cross Longmire-Paradise Road and continue hiking on the Wonderland Trail back to the Longmire Historic District. There are many signs to point the way on this last stretch.

Miles and Directions

0.0 Start at the Longmire Historic District. Cross the Longmire-Paradise Road; stay to the right until you reach the trailhead for the Trail of the Shadows. Enjoy the mineral springs, Longmire cabin, Iron Mike, and Travertine Mound exhibits before reaching the Rampart Ridge Trail junction.

0.5 At the junction with the Rampart Ridge Trail, go right (north).

2.2 A spur trail to the right goes to a viewpoint. Continue on the Rampart Ridge Trail, hiking northeast.

3.4 Arrive at the Wonderland Trail junction after traveling a little over a mile from the viewpoint. Go right (south) at this junction.

3.6 A trail that leads to Van Trump Park heads off to the left (northeast). Stay to the right, heading south.

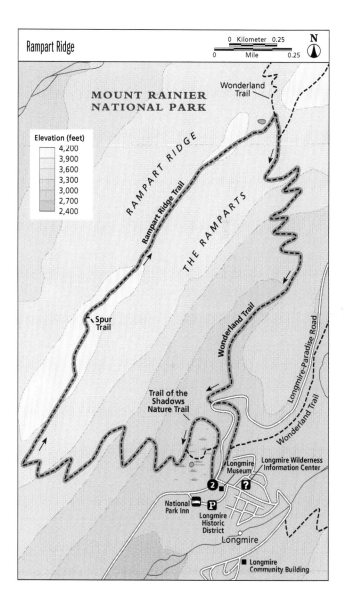

Rampart Ridge

Wonderland
Trail

MOUNT RAINIER
NATIONAL PARK

Elevation (feet)
4,200
3,900
3,600
3,300
3,000
2,700
2,400

RAMPART RIDGE

Rampart Ridge Trail

THE RAMPARTS

Spur
Trail

Wonderland Trail

Longmire-Paradise Road

Trail of the
Shadows
Nature Trail

Wonderland Trail

Longmire
Museum

Longmire Wilderness
Information Center

2

?

National
Park Inn

P

Longmire
Historic
District

Longmire

Longmire
Community Building

4.9 Cross the Longmire-Paradise Road and continue hiking on the Wonderland Trail. There are many signs to point the way on this last stretch.

5.1 Arrive back at the Longmire Historic District.

Option: If you are not in the mood for a history lesson, you can easily bypass the self-guided tour in the Trail of the Shadows by heading left (south) or clockwise on the Trail of the Shadows until you reach the Rampart Ridge Trail in 0.1 mile. This cuts off approximately half a mile from the total hike.

3 Trail of the Shadows

A 30-minute stroll encircling the Longmire Meadow, the Trail of the Shadows has attractions that provide information and facts about local flora and fauna, geological phenomena, and human exploration and extraction with an emphasis on the history and experience of the Longmire family.

Start: Longmire Historic District
Distance: 0.7-mile lollipop
Hiking time: 30 minutes
Trail surface: Well-maintained; forest floor
Elevation gain: Minimal
Best season: May through Oct
Nearest town: Ashford

Fees and permits: Vehicle or individual entry fee (7 days); annual entry available; timed entry applies
Trail contacts: Longmire Wilderness Information Center, (360) 569-6650

Finding the trailhead: From the Nisqually Entrance Station, drive 6.7 miles east on Longmire-Paradise Road. Look for the Longmire Historic District on the right (east). Park in one of the many spaces around the Longmire Wilderness Information Center, the Longmire Museum, and the National Park Inn, then cross the road along one of several crosswalks to find the trailhead toward the right (north) of the crosswalks. **GPS:** N46 45.013' / W121 48.786'

The Hike

The trail winds around an enchanting meadow while leading you to many informative stations. The trailside interpretive signs not only describe the area's history, but also the ecology of the meadow and surrounding forest and the geology of the mountain and the mineral springs.

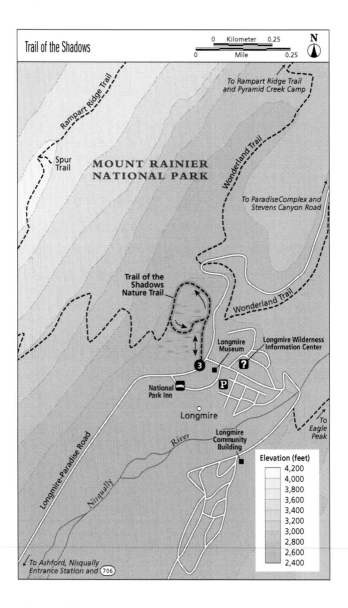

Trail of the Shadows

Mount Rainier National Park

To Rampart Ridge Trail and Pyramid Creek Camp

Rampart Ridge Trail

Spur Trail

Wonderland Trail

To ParadiseComplex and Stevens Canyon Road

Trail of the Shadows Nature Trail

Wonderland Trail

Longmire Museum

Longmire Wilderness Information Center

3

National Park Inn

P

Longmire

To Eagle Peak

Longmire Community Building

Longmire-Paradise Road

River

Nisqually

Elevation (feet)

| 4,200 |
| 4,000 |
| 3,800 |
| 3,600 |
| 3,400 |
| 3,200 |
| 3,000 |
| 2,800 |
| 2,600 |
| 2,400 |

To Ashford, Nisqually Entrance Station and 706

N

Starting to the right (north), the first stop is a work of stone masonry with bubbling water, said in the nineteenth century to cure any illness. As the sign ironically reads, do not drink this water. It can make you very ill. The next stop, 0.2 mile into the hike, is the Longmire cabin. Although every log, beam, and shingle has been replaced over the years, the cabin stands as an authentic replica of one built by James Longmire, an early pioneer who laid claim to the area. The park service has also placed in the cabin furniture reminiscent of the style of the day. Next door is Iron Mike, a spring that is tinted orange by iron minerals.

A very small side trip at 0.5 mile from the trailhead leads to the Travertine Mound, another orange mass bursting with mineral water. A bench here provides a nice place to sit and view the meadow.

The home stretch of the loop feels like a return to the Carboniferous Period, with its giant carbon-rich plants. The skunk cabbages rise the size of grown humans and massive Devil's Club protrudes with giant, thorny shoots. After completing the loop, cross the Longmire-Paradise Road again to get back to your car and the large present-day Longmire Historic District. Notice the great disparity between the present-day edifices and the shadows of the past.

Miles and Directions

0.0 Start at the Longmire Historic District. Cross the road along one of the two crosswalks to find the trailhead.

0.1 You're standing before the masonry spring.

0.2 Pass Longmire's cabin and very quickly come to Iron Mike.

0.5 A small spur trail takes you to the Travertine Mound.

0.7 Arrive back at the trailhead. Head back across the road to the Longmire Historic District.

4 Carter Falls

An early opener, this portion of the Wonderland Trail crosses the expansive Nisqually River basin and skirts the Paradise River on its mild ascent to a treed-in vista of Carter Falls.

Start: Carter Falls Trailhead (Wonderland Trail across from Cougar Rock Campground)

Distance: 2.5 miles out and back

Hiking time: 1.5-2 hours

Trail surface: Well-maintained; begins in rocky river basin and transitions to dirt forest floor

Elevation gain: 1,200 feet

Best season: Mid-June through Oct

Nearest town: Ashford

Fees and permits: Vehicle or individual entry fee (7 days); annual entry available; timed entry applies

Trail contacts: Longmire Wilderness Information Center, (360) 569-6650

Finding the trailhead: From the Nisqually Entrance Station, drive east on Longmire-Paradise Road. At 6.7 miles, you pass the Longmire Historic District on the right (east). Continue another 2.5 miles, where you come to two pullouts, the first on the left side of the road, and the second on the right (east) with a viewpoint over the Nisqually River. If you reach Cougar Rock Campground, you have just passed them. Park in either of these pullouts and head toward the viewpoint. The trail starts on the south side of the parking area with the viewpoint and heads down into the river basin. **GPS:** N46 45.990' / W121 47.464'

The Hike

Situated between the Longmire Historic District and the Paradise area and originating near a popular campground, the Carter Falls Trail sees many visitors. Throngs of tourists meander along the rocks in the Nisqually River basin waiting for that ephemeral glimpse of Mount Rainier. The Carter Falls Trail is particularly popular in early summer, when the snow in Paradise has not yet melted and trail choices are limited. Admittedly, Carter Falls is an unlikely destination for many hikers, as its jetting waters are hardly visible through the trees, but the hike has many other qualities to offer: a massive glacier river basin, an unobstructed view of Mount Rainier on a clear day, a relatively easy grade, and early accessibility.

From the trailhead, descend into the Nisqually River basin for 0.2 mile until you reach a log footbridge over the river. If the log footbridge over the Nisqually River is out, find another hike. Glacial rivers have a high concentration of debris and there is a risk of large glacial boulders being in the water.

If the bridge is intact, cross the bridge and follow the well-marked trail into the woods. Eagle Peak, the westernmost peak in the Tatoosh Range, rises above you to the south, and sits directly in front of you for a brief part of the hike. The trail makes a U-shape, at first heading south toward Eagle Peak until it reaches a small bluff, and then turning north before finally settling on its eastbound trajectory along the Paradise River. The cool waters of the Paradise River once originated from the Paradise Glacier and tumbled over Narada Falls before reaching this point. Since the major recession of the Paradise Glacier, the river is fed by snowmelt and springs from the Paradise area and the northern slope of the Tatoosh Range. Massive boulders and fallen trees dot the river, as you ascend gradually to the falls. The large pipe seen along the trail is a historic wooden water-supply pipe made of cedar wood and steel support rings that once fed water to

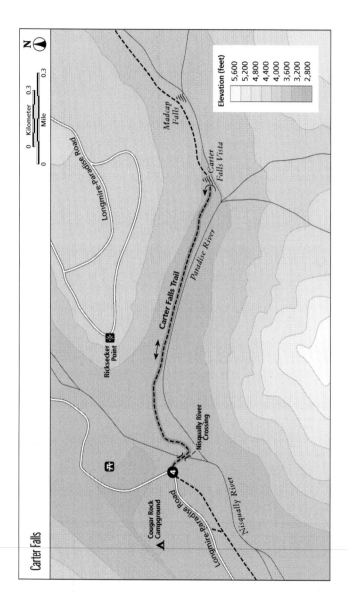

Carter Falls

N

Cougar Rock Campground ▲

Longmire-Paradise Road

Nisqually River

Nisqually River Crossing

Carter Falls Trail

Ricksecker Point

Longmire-Paradise Road

Paradise River

Carter Falls Vista

Madcap Falls

0   Kilometer   0.3

0   Mile

Elevation (feet)
5,600
5,200
4,800
4,400
4,000
3,600
3,200
2,800

an old hydroelectric power plant that once stood next to the trail alongside the Paradise River. The trail ascends gradually along this pipe all the way to Carter Falls.

Miles and Directions

0.0 Start at the Carter Falls Trailhead, and travel a portion of the Wonderland Trail. Descend into the Nisqually River basin along the well-marked and well-maintained trail.

0.2 Cross the Nisqually River over the log footbridge and head into the forest.

1.25 You reach Carter Falls, as you know from a sign posted along the trail, the sound of rushing water, and a view through the trees. Return the way you came.

2.5 Arrive back at the trailhead.

Option: Just 100 yards up the way from Carter Falls is a second waterfall, Madcap Falls, which affords a clearer and more interesting view. We strongly recommend that you take the extra steps to get there.

5 Comet Falls

A craggy climb past water features and pika–filled rock fields to the foot of Comet Falls. Named for the water's likeness to a comet's tail, it plunges 320 feet into the creek below and is one of the tallest falls in the park.

Start: Van Trump Park Trailhead (otherwise known as the Comet Falls Trailhead)
Distance: 3.8 miles out and back
Hiking time: 2.5-4 hours
Trail surface: Well-maintained; begins on forest floor with large roots and switches to a rocky trail
Elevation gain: 2,160 feet
Best season: Mid-July through Sept

Nearest town: Ashford
Fees and permits: Vehicle or individual entry fee (7 days); annual entry available; timed entry applies
Trail contacts: Longmire Wilderness Information Center, (360) 569-6650
Special considerations: The Van Trump Park Trailhead offers limited parking that is often overcrowded in peak season.

Finding the trailhead: From the Nisqually Entrance Station, drive 10.7 miles east on Longmire-Paradise Road. The parking lot is on your left. **GPS:** N46 46.754' / W121 46.958'

The Hike

The trail takes you through beautiful forest to several waterfalls, including spectacular Comet Falls, one of the tallest falls in the park.

From the Van Trump Park Trail parking lot, hike north on the Van Trump Park Trail. The hike starts off with a bang, as you reach a bridge crossing Christine Falls in less than

0.3 mile. The bridge provides a bird's-eye view of the oft-photographed falls that roar and churn around granite walls until making their final tumble near the Longmire-Paradise Road.

After Christine Falls, the trail first traverses the forest via switchbacks, then hugs the hillside over Van Trump Creek, and finally opens up to fields of rock and talus in its approach to Comet Falls. This hike proves more difficult than its length and pitch would indicate, as trail hazards are common. In the trees, roots are major trip hazards, while the large rocky steps of the upper trail make this hike harder than expected. Similarly, the myriad flora lining the trail change as you climb. Just after the snow has melted completely from the trail, trillium, red columbine, tiger lily, and goatsbeard dominate in the lower elevation, giving way to fields of salmon berries and eventually avalanche lilies near the falls.

Just before you reach the first viewpoint of Comet Falls, you come to a bridge over Van Trump Creek with an unnamed falls to your right (east). The trail seems to fork before the bridge, but stay to the left (north). The trail to the right is a small spur trail that wraps around the bend to the foot of the unnamed falls. You have a nice view of the falls from the bridge and its surrounding rocks. These boulders provide the most comfortable lunch spot on the trail; the area around Comet Falls is not as conducive to a relaxing break.

You reach your first view of Comet Falls 1.7 miles from the beginning of your hike, but several viewing areas await you in the next 0.2 mile of steep switchbacks to a close-up, and likely wet, view of your destination. The white waters of Comet Falls resemble the tail of a comet, the inspiration for its name, as they plunge 320 feet into the creek below.

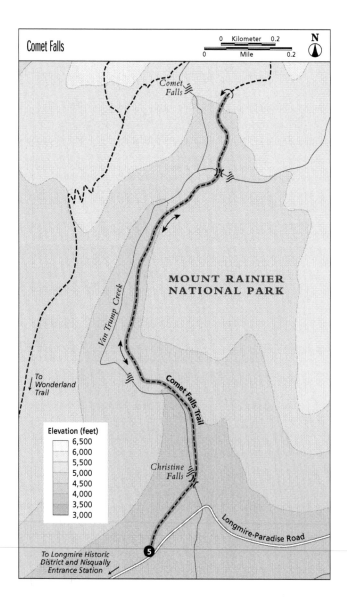

Comet Falls

0   Kilometer   0.2

0   Mile   0.2

N

Comet Falls

MOUNT RAINIER NATIONAL PARK

Van Trump Creek

To Wonderland Trail

Comet Falls Trail

Elevation (feet)

6,500
6,000
5,500
5,000
4,500
4,000
3,500
3,000

Christine Falls

Longmire-Paradise Road

To Longmire Historic District and Nisqually Entrance Station

5

Miles and Directions

0.0 Start at the Van Trump Park Trailhead (sometimes referred to as Comet Falls Trailhead). Travel north up the Van Trump Park Trail.

0.3 A bridge over Christine Falls offers you a bird's-eye view of its churning waters.

1.6 An unnamed falls appears to your right (east) as you cross a footbridge over Van Trump Creek before making your final ascent to Comet Falls.

1.9 After several viewing opportunities along the switchbacks to Comet Falls, you reach your closest vista of the 320-foot waterfall. When ready to return, just retrace your steps.

3.8 Arrive back at the trailhead.

6 Alta Vista Summit

This short hike travels steeply through beautiful meadows overlooking the Paradise area.

Start: Lower parking lot of Paradise
Distance: 1.6-mile lollipop
Hiking time: 1 hour
Trail surface: Well-maintained; subalpine meadow, largely paved
Elevation gain: Minimal
Best season: Early July through Sept
Nearest towns: Ashford or Packwood

Fees and permits: Vehicle or individual entry fee (7 days); annual entry available; timed entry applies
Trail contacts: Henry M. Jackson Memorial Visitor Center at Paradise, (360) 569-6571
Special considerations: Parking at the Paradise Complex can be hard to find. Come mid-week or off-season for the best chance of finding a spot.

Finding the trailhead: From the Nisqually Entrance Station, travel 16 miles east on Longmire-Paradise Road. Stay to the left (north) where the road forks, following the signs to Paradise. From the Stevens Canyon Entrance Station, travel nearly 19 miles on Stevens Canyon Road to the intersection with Longmire-Paradise Road. Turn right (north) and follow the signs to Paradise. Make your first left into the lower parking lot, which is designated for more than two-hour stays, and find a spot. The trail originates from the middle of lower parking lot and heads northeast. **GPS:** N46 47.076' / W121 44.464'

The Hike

This hike is excellent for children able to troop up a decent hill. It is short and scenic and gives you a little taste of Mount Rainier National Park. If you take this hike in July or August,

an abundance of wildflowers will line your path. Please preserve the fragile meadows where the flowers grow by staying
on the trail. Expect to see a lot of people on this popular trail.

This well-traveled and well-maintained trail heads northeast from the center of the lower parking lot.

Continue 0.1 mile north on the Alta Vista Trail to the
Avalanche Lily Trail junction, which runs west to the Dead
Horse Creek Trail. Go straight for another 0.2 mile and
come to the Waterfall Trail intersection. Again, head straight
(north) along the Alta Vista Trail. Very shortly, you reach the
intersection with the Skyline Trail; stay on your current trail,
heading north toward the Alta Vista Summit. Despite the
trail congestion in this area, detailed signs help you continue
north on the Alta Vista Trail. After the intersection with the
Skyline Trail, the grade turns markedly steep. Pace yourself.

About 0.5 mile into your hike, you come to the beginning of the loop to the Alta Vista Summit. Go left (northwest) and uphill toward the summit with the help of a sign
that points you in the correct direction. Below, Paradise Park
is to the right (east). You can see many people milling about
below you on other Paradise trails. Turn around and look
to the south for a fabulous view of the jutting peaks of the
Tatoosh Range.

If you need a rest, enjoy the view from one of the many
rock benches along the trail. Please preserve the meadows by
staying on the trail or in a designated rest area.

When you have enjoyed yourself to the fullest, complete
the loop by continuing north on the Alta Vista Trail and
turning right (southeast) onto the east side of the loop in
about 0.1 mile, or simply turn around and go back the way
you came. Turn right and head south on the east side of the
Alta Vista Trail until the loop rejoins itself, 1 mile into your

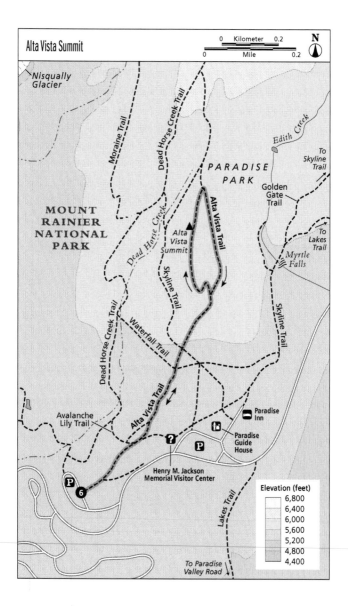

Alta Vista Summit

Nisqually
Glacier

Moraine Trail

Dead Horse Creek Trail

Dead Horse Creek

MOUNT
RAINIER
NATIONAL
PARK

PARADISE
PARK

Edith Creek

To
Skyline
Trail

Golden
Gate
Trail

To
Lakes
Trail

Myrtle
Falls

Alta Vista Trail

Alta
Vista
Summit

Skyline Trail

Skyline Trail

Waterfall Trail

Dead Horse Creek Trail

Alta Vista Trail

Avalanche
Lily Trail

Paradise
Inn

Paradise
Guide
House

Henry M. Jackson
Memorial Visitor Center

P

6

Lakes Trail

To Paradise
Valley Road

Kilometer   0.2

0

0   Mile   0.2

N

Elevation (feet)
6,800
6,400
6,000
5,600
5,200
4,800
4,400

hike. From this point, head back down the trail to the parking lot.

Miles and Directions

0.0 The top portion of the lower parking lot loop is home to two trailheads, the Nisqually Vista Trail and the Alta Vista Trail. Head northeast on the Alta Vista Trail from the center of the lot.

0.1 At the junction with the Avalanche Lily Trail, which connects the upper parking lot with the Dead Horse Creek Trail, stay straight ahead on the Alta Vista Trail.

0.2 Again, stay the course (north) at the junction with the Waterfall Trail, which connects the Skyline Trail to the Dead Horse Creek Trail. Shortly thereafter, you come to the Skyline Trail junction; again stay straight (north) on the Alta Vista Trail.

0.5 The loop of the lollipop begins. Take a left (west) at the fork, following the signs for Alta Vista Summit. Notice Paradise Park down below you to the northeast and the myriad hikers on other trails in the area.

1.1 Complete the loop; stay to the left (south) at the stem of the lollipop.

1.6 Arrive back at the lower parking lot.

7 Nisqually Vista

This short hike travels through picturesque subalpine forest and meadow to an overlook with expansive views of the Nisqually Glacier and Mount Rainier.

Start: Dead Horse Creek Trailhead
Distance: 1.2-mile lollipop
Hiking time: 1 hour
Trail surface: Well-maintained; paved
Elevation gain: Minimal
Best season: Early July through Sept
Nearest towns: Ashford or Packwood

Fees and permits: Vehicle or individual entry fee (7 days); annual entry available; timed entry applies
Trail contacts: Henry M. Jackson Memorial Visitor Center at Paradise, (360) 569-6571
Special considerations: Parking at the Paradise Complex can be difficult. Come mid-week or off-season for the best chance of finding a spot.

Finding the trailhead: From the Nisqually Entrance Station, travel 16 miles east on Longmire-Paradise Road. Stay to the left (north) where the road forks, following the signs to Paradise. From the Stevens Canyon Entrance Station, travel nearly 19 miles on Stevens Canyon Road to the intersection with Longmire-Paradise Road. Turn right (north) and follow the signs to Paradise. Make your first left into the lower parking lot, which is designated for more than two-hour stays.
GPS: N46 47.103' / W121 44.496'

The Hike

This is a great hike for kids and adults alike. Entirely paved, it is suitable for strollers. However, getting a wheelchair up the first few steps might be a challenge. No matter your age or abilities, Nisqually Vista takes you through beautiful, forested areas and wonderful subalpine meadows to several viewpoints overlooking the Nisqually Glacier. The Nisqually Vista Trail is a self-guiding trail, but the National Park Service offers a guided tour of this hike in summer and leads snowshoe walks throughout winter. Inquire at the Henry M. Jackson Visitor Center for more information. It is downhill all the way to the lookout and then uphill back to the parking lot, but both gradients are gradual.

To begin the hike, go to the northwest end of the lower-level parking lot. Look for a larger sign and step to a trailhead post for the Nisqually Vista and Dead Horse Creek Trail. Stay toward the left (northwest), and take the Nisqually Vista Trail, which branches off very near the inception of the hike. In less than 0.3 mile the trail forks again. This fork marks the beginning of the loop section of this lollipop. You could go either way. We recommend heading left (west) on the Nisqually Vista Trail and hiking the loop clockwise. Halfway through the loop, and halfway through your hike, you come to a viewpoint. There are three viewpoints, and the first one has a display on the Nisqually Glacier.

From all the viewpoints you can see where the Nisqually River's headwaters flow from the Nisqually Glacier and the massive moraine kicked up by eons of glacial movement.

The rest of the loop is a little over 0.3 mile long and takes you through quaint forest with meadows of lupine and pasqueflower. When you come to the end of the loop, stay to the left, back toward the parking lot. Enjoy a leisurely return trip.

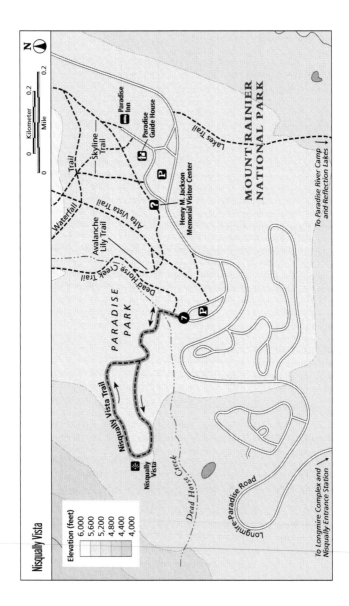

Nisqually Vista

Elevation (feet)

6,000
5,600
5,200
4,800
4,400
4,000

N

0   Kilometer   0.2

0   Mile   0.2

Waterfall

Trail

Skyline Trail

Avalanche Lily Trail

Alta Vista Trail

Dead Horse Creek Trail

PARADISE PARK

Nisqually Vista Trail

Nisqually Vista

Dead Horse Creek

Longmire-Paradise Road

Paradise Inn

Paradise Guide House

P

Henry M. Jackson Memorial Visitor Center

?

P

Lakes Trail

MOUNT RAINIER NATIONAL PARK

To Paradise River Camp and Reflection Lakes

To Longmire Complex and Nisqually Entrance Station

Miles and Directions

0.0 Start heading to the northwest end of the lower parking lot. Look for a trail sign for the Dead Horse Creek Trail with a set of stairs. Stay toward the left (northwest), and take the Nisqually Vista Trail, which branches off very near the inception of the hike.

0.3 Nisqually Vista Trail forks at the loop part of the lollipop trail. Stay to the left (west), following the Nisqually Vista Trail.

0.6 Halfway through the hike, come to the first viewpoint of the Nisqually Glacier, the Nisqually River, and the moraine; the viewpoint provides an informational display. Two more viewpoints follow in quick succession.

0.9 End of loop; stay to the left (east) on the Nisqually Vista Trail.

1.2 At the Dead Horse Creek Trailhead, the hike is basically over; you can see the lower parking lot.

8 Dead Horse Creek

This short, paved spur trail meanders through meadow to the Skyline Trail and offers great views of the Tatoosh Range, Mount Rainier, and the Nisqually Glacier.

Start: Dead Horse Creek Trail (Paradise area lower parking lot)
Distance: 2.2 miles out and back
Hiking time: 1-2 hours
Trail surface: Well-maintained; forest and subalpine meadow
Elevation gain: 600 feet
Best season: July through Sept

Nearest towns: Ashford or Packwood
Fees and permits: Vehicle or individual entry fee (7 days); annual entry available; timed entry applies
Trail contacts: Henry M. Jackson Memorial Visitor Center at Paradise, (360) 569-6571

Finding the trailhead: From the Nisqually Entrance Station, drive nearly 16 miles east on Longmire-Paradise Road to where it intersects with the Stevens Canyon Road (and the turnoff for the Ohanapecosh area). Rather than heading toward Ohanapecosh, follow the signs to Paradise and stay to the left (north) along the Longmire-Paradise Road for another 2.1 miles. From the Stevens Canyon Entrance Station, travel nearly 19 miles on Stevens Canyon Road to the intersection with Longmire-Paradise Road. Turn right (north) and follow the signs to Paradise. Make your first left into the lower parking lot, which is designated for more than two-hour stays. **GPS:** N46 47.103' / W121 44.496'

The Hike

A shorter, paved, and more gradual alternative to the Skyline Trail, Dead Horse Creek Trail winds over Paradise meadows and affords awesome views of Mount Rainier and the

Tatoosh Range. In July and August wildflowers like western anemone, lupine, paintbrush, and Lewis's monkeyflower line your path. Listen for the hooting call of sooty grouse who bed in the abundant flora. Please preserve their splendid home by staying on designated trails.

To start the hike, head to the northwest end of the lower-level parking lot. Look for a trail sign for the Dead Horse Creek Trail. Stay to the right, heading north on the Dead Horse Creek Trail. The trail first takes you through serene subalpine forest. Although the Paradise area has extremely high traffic, this trail receives less use than others in the area.

Continue north on the Dead Horse Creek Trail, ignoring the two trails that come in from the right at 0.1 mile (the Avalanche Lily Trail) and 0.4 mile (the Waterfall Trail). Both of these trails travel to the Paradise Ranger Station and the Paradise Inn. At every intersection a sign bears directions to help you stay on the Dead Horse Creek Trail. The Nisqually Glacier lies to the west. The National Park Service has set up several rock benches from which to enjoy the view. Please use the provided benches to minimize your impact on the fragile subalpine meadows.

The Moraine Trail intersects the Dead Horse Creek Trail from the left at 0.7 mile. Stay to the right (northeast), unless you plan to take the Moraine Trail option. Not far from the junction with the Moraine Trail, a small spur trail branches off to the right, connecting with the Skyline Trail. Stay on the main trail.

The trail is considerably steeper at this point, but you have only 0.4 mile to the end of the trail, over a mile into your hike. The end of Dead Horse Creek Trail is the Skyline Trail. You have the option of hiking back down the way you just came or making a loop by following the Skyline Trail. If

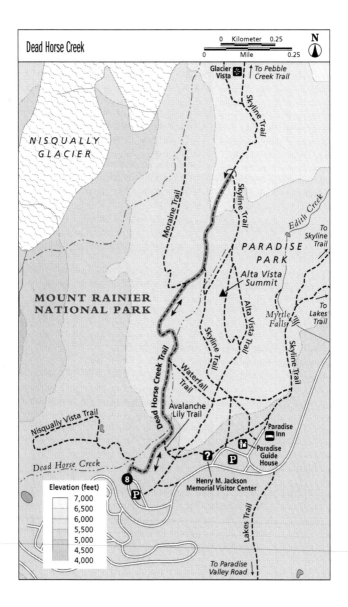

Dead Horse Creek

Glacier
Vista

To Pebble
Creek Trail

Skyline Trail

NISQUALLY
GLACIER

Moraine Trail

Skyline Trail

Edith Creek

To
Skyline
Trail

PARADISE
PARK

Alta Vista
Summit

MOUNT RAINIER
NATIONAL PARK

Myrtle
Falls

To
Lakes
Trail

Alta Vista Trail

Skyline Trail

Skyline Trail

Dead Horse Creek Trail

Waterfall
Trail

Avalanche
Lily Trail

Nisqually Vista Trail

Dead Horse Creek

Paradise
Inn

Paradise
Guide
House

8

P

Henry M. Jackson
Memorial Visitor Center

P

Lakes Trail

Elevation (feet)

7,000
6,500
6,000
5,500
5,000
4,500
4,000

To Paradise
Valley Road

you choose to take the Skyline Trail, follow the signs back to the visitor center.

Miles and Directions

0.0   Start by heading to the west end of the lower parking lot. Look for a trail sign for the Dead Horse Creek Trail and stay to the right, heading north.

0.1   When the Avalanche Lily Trail comes in from the right (east), continue straight (north) on the Dead Horse Creek Trail.

0.4   Pass the junction with the Waterfall Trail, which heads toward the Paradise Inn and continue hiking north on the Dead Horse Creek Trail.

0.7   The Moraine Trail spurs off to the left. If you want to see the Nisqually Glacier up close, you can take this option and add a mile of trail to your hiking time. Otherwise, stay to the right (northeast) along the Dead Horse Creek Trail. Also stay on the main trail when encountered with the connector to the Skyline Trail in just a few paces.

1.1   The Skyline Trail junction marks the end of the Dead Horse Creek Trail. Turn around (south) and return the way you came.

2.2   Arrive back at the trailhead.

⑨ High Lakes Trail

This short loop around Reflection Lakes offers a great view of the Tatoosh Range to the south, and when the weather is right, a prime spot to photograph Mount Rainier mirrored in the still lake waters.

Start: Reflection Lakes
Distance: 2.7-mile loop
Hiking time: 1.5-2 hours
Trail surface: Well-maintained; forest floor
Elevation gain: Minimal
Best season: July through Sept
Nearest towns: Ashford or Packwood

Fees and permits: Vehicle or individual entry fee (7 days); annual entry available; timed entry applies
Trail contacts: Henry M. Jackson Memorial Visitor Center at Paradise, (360) 569-6571

Finding the trailhead: From Stevens Canyon Entrance Station, drive nearly 18 miles on Stevens Canyon Road to Reflection Lakes. From the Nisqually Entrance Station, travel nearly 16 miles east on Longmire-Paradise Road to the turnoff for the Ohanapecosh area. Turn right (southeast) onto Stevens Canyon Road and toward Ohanapecosh. Stay on this road for just under a mile. Reflection Lakes hosts a string of parking spaces on the left (north) side of the road. The High Lakes Trailhead technically starts in the middle of these parking spots, but you can access the trail all along the loop as well. **GPS:** N46 46.112' / W121 43.883'

The Hike

This easy day hike explores the area around Reflection Lakes, possibly the most photographed spot on Mount Rainier. Aptly named, on a clear day you can see the entire mountain mirrored in the still waters of Reflection Lakes. The High Lakes Trail leaves the lakeside and follows Mazama Ridge, gaining just enough elevation to afford a view of the Tatoosh Range.

We recommend hiking this loop counterclockwise to minimize the abruptness of your elevation gain. From the Reflection Lakes parking lot, walk east along Stevens Canyon Road until you reach the junction with the Wonderland Trail toward Louise Lake. Go left (northeast) onto the Lakes Trail, leaving the Wonderland Trail behind. Continue on the Lakes Trail up the south side of Mazama Ridge—a relatively steep but short section—to the High Lakes Trail, 0.7 mile into your hike.

Turn left (west) onto the High Lakes Trail. This trail is mostly downhill or flat, with many opportunities to view the Tatoosh Range and three of its jagged pinnacles—Pinnacle, Plummer, and Unicorn Peaks—jutting above the horizon.

After 1.2 miles the High Lakes Trail rejoins the Lakes Trail. Go left (south) and downhill on the lower Lakes Trail for 0.5 mile to a junction with the Wonderland Trail. Stay to the left and head toward Reflection Lakes for the next 0.2 mile to Stevens Canyon Road. Walk 0.1 mile east along the road back to where you parked.

Miles and Directions

0.0   Start from the Reflection Lakes parking lot. Walk east along Stevens Canyon Road until you reach the junction with the Wonderland Trail toward Louise Lake.

0.3   The Wonderland Trail diverges from the Lakes Trail to head toward Louise Lake. Stay left (north) on the Lakes Trail and head up Mazama Ridge.

High Lakes Trail

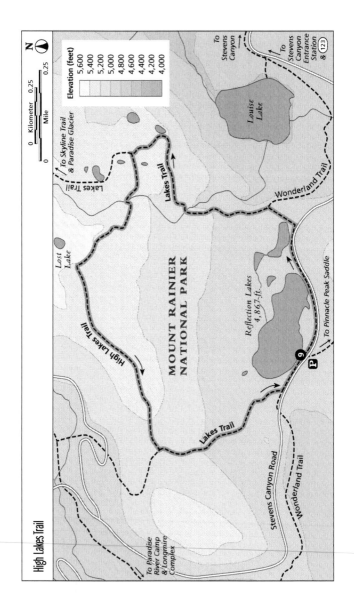

N

Elevation (feet)	
	5,600
	5,400
	5,200
	5,000
	4,800
	4,600
	4,400
	4,200
	4,000

0   Kilometer   0.25

0   Mile   0.25

To Skyline Trail
& Paradise Glacier

Lakes Trail

Lakes Trail

To Stevens Canyon

To Stevens
Canyon
Entrance
Station
& 123

Louise Lake

Lakes Trail

Lost Lake

High Lakes Trail

Wonderland Trail

MOUNT RAINIER
NATIONAL PARK

Reflection Lakes
4,867-ft.

To Pinnacle Peak Saddle

P
9

Lakes Trail

Stevens Canyon Road

Wonderland Trail

To Paradise
River Camp
& Longmire
Complex

0.7 At the High Lakes Trail junction, make sure you take a left (west) onto High Lakes. Otherwise, you could follow the Lakes Trail all the way to Paradise.

1.9 When you reach the Lakes Trail junction, you have completed the top section of the loop known as the High Lakes Trail. Stay to the left (south) on the Lakes Trail to get back to your car.

2.4 Once again, the Wonderland Trail intersects the Lakes Trail. Stay to the left (southeast) toward the Reflection Lakes parking lot.

2.7 Arrive back at the Reflection Lakes trailhead.

10 **Pinnacle Peak Saddle**

This short, rocky climb up to the saddle between Pinnacle and Plummer Peaks offers great views of the south flank of Mount Rainier to the north and Mount Adams and Mount St. Helens to the south.

Start: Pinnacle Peak Trailhead, across from Reflection Lakes
Distance: 2.6 miles out and back
Hiking time: 1.5–2 hours
Trail surface: Well-maintained; forest floor, rocky, scree
Elevation gain: 1,000 feet
Best season: Late July through Sept

Nearest towns: Ashford or Packwood
Fees and permits: Vehicle or individual entry fee (7 days); annual entry available; timed entry applies
Trail contacts: Henry M. Jackson Memorial Visitor Center at Paradise, (360) 569-6571

Finding the trailhead: From Stevens Canyon Entrance Station, drive nearly 18 miles on Stevens Canyon Road to Reflection Lakes. From the Nisqually Entrance Station, travel nearly 16 miles east on Longmire-Paradise Road to the turnoff for the Ohanapecosh area. Turn right (southeast) onto Stevens Canyon Road and toward Ohanapecosh. Stay on this road for just under a mile. Reflection Lakes hosts a string of parking spaces. The well-marked trailhead to Pinnacle Peak starts opposite the middle lot. **GPS:** N46 46.095' / W121 43.869'

The Hike

There are no tricky turns or trail junctions on this hike, just a steady ascent to the saddle between Pinnacle and Plummer Peaks. Simply head south from the trailhead, directly across from the busy Reflection Lakes parking lot, and hike all the way to the saddle. The first half of the trail runs through forest, blooming with lilies and lupine in the early season and abounding with delicious huckleberries in late summer. Gentiana clusters along the trail on occasion and monkey-flower grows near the occasional stream.

You climb steadily toward the saddle, but once you hit the first scree field, the trail becomes very rocky, making the ascent feel steeper and more precarious. Snow can linger on these rock fields late into summer—waterproof hiking boots are the footwear of choice here if you prefer to keep your toes dry.

Once you leave the trees for good, the talus fields start to dominate the landscape and the ancient crags of the Tatoosh peaks rise above them. Pikas can be heard chirping from their stone homes, and you may spot a marmot sunning itself on a warm rock. Heather and bear grass cling to the rocky soil.

There are just two switchbacks before you begin the final push to the saddle, the first of which may very well boast the best view of the hike. The Paradise Complex sits across the valley, with its visitor center, inn, crisscrossing trails, and climbers marching in step toward Camp Muir. The Nisqually Glacier pours down from the summit and nestles her nose in the riverbed she blazed. Around the second switchback and you are nearly home-free. Pinnacle Peak looms to your left as you round a cliff to reach the designated saddle. A bat cave carved into this rock wall shelters brown bats.

When you reach ridgeline, you can see to the south boundary of the park and all the way to Packwood. Mount Adams stands to the southeast, and Mount St. Helens sits a headless mirror on the opposite side of your panorama (southwest). Unmaintained spur trails dart left (east) and right

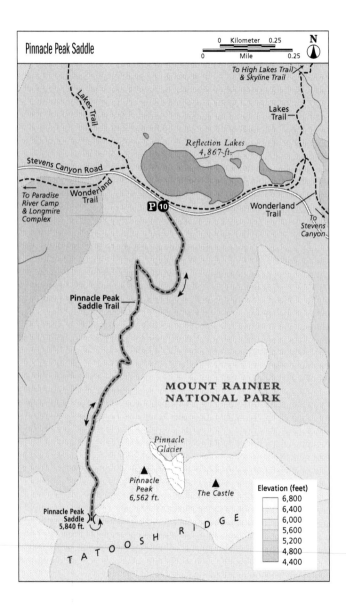

Pinnacle Peak Saddle

0   Kilometer   0.25

0   Mile   0.25

N

To High Lakes Trail
& Skyline Trail

Lakes Trail

Lakes
Trail

Reflection Lakes
4,867 ft.

Stevens Canyon Road

Wonderland
Trail

P 10

Wonderland
Trail

To Paradise
River Camp
& Longmire
Complex

To
Stevens
Canyon

Pinnacle Peak
Saddle Trail

MOUNT RAINIER
NATIONAL PARK

Pinnacle
Glacier

Pinnacle
Peak
6,562 ft.

The Castle

Elevation (feet)

6,800
6,400
6,000
5,600
5,200
4,800
4,400

Pinnacle Peak
Saddle
5,840 ft.

TATOOSH   RIDGE

(west). For a closer vantage of Plummer and Denman Peak, head west and explore a bit. Those with climbing expertise and equipment may turn west and tackle a summit of Pinnacle Peak or the Castle.

Otherwise, enjoy the amazing view before heading back the way you came.

Miles and Directions

0.0 Start heading south from the Pinnacle Peak Trailhead, across Stevens Canyon Road from Reflection Lakes.

1.3 Reach the Pinnacle Peak Saddle. Head back the way you came, or opt for the scramble to the top.

2.6 Arrive back at the trailhead.

Option: The maintained trail ends 1.3 miles into the hike, but there are unmaintained trails heading along the ridges of both Pinnacle and Plummer Peaks. The scramble up to Pinnacle Peak is hazardous and should be approached with caution.

11 Paradise Glacier

This route begins on the paved Skyline Trail, turns onto an unmaintained trail, and terminates at a glacial moraine that once brought explorers to its ice caves.

Start: Skyline Trailhead
Distance: 6.2 miles out and back
Hiking time: 3–4 hours
Trail surface: Well-maintained; paved and subalpine meadow to unmaintained trail
Elevation gain: 1,000 feet
Best season: Mid-July through Sept
Nearest towns: Ashford or Packwood
Fees and permits: Vehicle or individual entry fee (7 days); annual entry available; timed entry applies
Trail contacts: Henry M. Jackson Memorial Visitor Center at Paradise, (360) 569-6571
Special considerations: Parking at the Paradise Complex can be difficult. Come mid-week or off-season for the best chance of finding a spot. The Paradise Glacier Trail is no longer maintained by the National Park Service, but crews do check regularly on the cairns.

Finding the trailhead: From the Nisqually Entrance Station, travel 16 miles east on Longmire-Paradise Road. Stay to the left (north) where the road forks, following the signs to Paradise. From the Stevens Canyon Entrance Station, travel nearly 19 miles on Stevens Canyon Road to the intersection with Longmire-Paradise Road. Turn right (north) and follow the signs to Paradise. Make your first left into the lower parking lot, which is designated for more than two-hour stays. Walk along the sidewalk toward the upper parking lot and the Henry M. Jackson Memorial Visitor Center. The northbound trail begins directly behind the visitor center. **GPS:** N46 47.216' / W121 44.071'

The Hike

The ice caves that once drew many to this trail have melted with the general increase in global temperature. This means a less sensational hike, but it also means fewer passersby and the same spectacular views as before.

Start hiking along the Skyline Trail via the trailhead directly behind the visitor center. Proceed to the right (east). Many trails congest this area, but just follow the Skyline Trail signs eastbound and you will reach your destination.

Hike gradually uphill along a wide, paved trail for just under 0.5 mile to arrive at Myrtle Falls. The path to the bottom of the falls is short but steep and offers a closer look. Back on the main trail, cross Edith Creek, the source of Myrtle Falls; stay to the right beyond the Golden Gate Trail junction.

Climb steadily, through occasional switchbacks, for 0.5 mile to the 4th Crossing Trail. Stay to the left, continuing east. Much like previous parts of the trail, this is a medium ascent through subalpine forest. You soon reach the Lakes Trail junction, 1.3 miles into the hike. Again, stay to the left, heading northeast.

The trail turns to head north; 0.4 mile after the Lakes Trail junction, look for a stone bench at a fork in the trail. This firm resting spot was erected by the Mountaineers and the Mazamas as a tribute to Hazard Stevens and Philemon Beecher Van Trump. The monument marks the campsite from which the two made the first recorded ascent of Mount Rainier, where their Yakama guide, Sluiskin, reluctantly agreed to wait two nights for their return. It also marks the Paradise Glacier Trail junction.

Turn right (northeast) onto the Paradise Glacier Trail. From here the ascent is gradual, but it leads into alpine terrain. Even in late summer be prepared to encounter snow; wear boots if you have them. The trail becomes fainter as you progress toward what once marked the Paradise Glacier and its popular ice caves. Cairns guide you beyond the terminus of the trail.

Mountain goats frequent this area, seeking refuge from the throngs of tourists on the more popular trails. They ramble over the rocky outcroppings that hem in the headwaters of Stevens Creek. If you do not spot them on the cliffs to your east, they may be just around the corner on the smooth, glaciated bedrock to your left (northwest). Either way, you can pull out your map and study Mount Rainier's south-flowing glaciers or turn around (south) for an arresting view of the Tatoosh Range, the Goat Rocks, and Mount Adams. When you are ready, return to Paradise along the same trail.

Miles and Directions

0.0 Start hiking to the right (east) along the Skyline Trail, which begins directly behind the visitor center in the northwestern corner of the parking lot.

0.4 Less than half a mile into your hike, come to a small trail to Myrtle Falls on your right (south) and the Golden Gate Trail junction on your left (north). You can take a peek at the falls, but come back to the Skyline Trail and continue east.

0.9 Reach the 4th Crossing Trail junction; stay to the left (east) along the Skyline Trail.

1.3 Stay to the left at the Lakes Trail junction.

1.7 When you spy a surreal rocky sofa in the middle of the trail, you know you have reached the Van Trump Monument

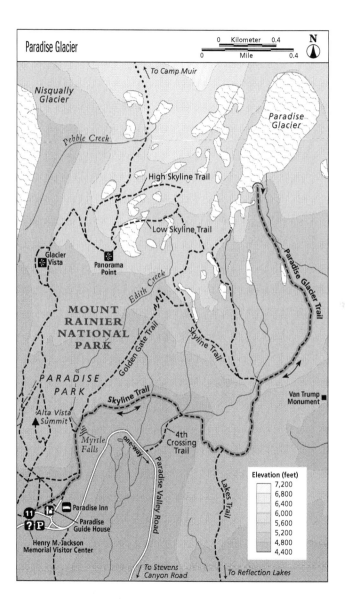

Paradise Glacier

Nisqually Glacier

Paradise Glacier

To Camp Muir

Pebble Creek

High Skyline Trail

Low Skyline Trail

Glacier Vista

Panorama Point

Paradise Glacier Trail

Edith Creek

MOUNT RAINIER NATIONAL PARK

Golden Gate Trail

Skyline Trail

PARADISE PARK

Skyline Trail

Van Trump Monument

Alta Vista Summit

Myrtle Falls

one-way

4th Crossing Trail

Paradise Valley Road

Lakes Trail

Paradise Inn

Paradise Guide House

Henry M. Jackson Memorial Visitor Center

To Stevens Canyon Road

To Reflection Lakes

Elevation (feet)

7,200
6,800
6,400
6,000
5,600
5,200
4,800
4,400

0   Kilometer   0.4
0   Mile   0.4

N

junction and the Paradise Glacier Trail junction. Take the Paradise Glacier Trail to your right (northeast).

3.1 Arrive at Paradise Glacier. After exploring the snowfield, return the way you came.

6.2 Arrive back at the trailhead.

12 Skyline Trail

Quite possibly the most popular hike in Mount Rainier National Park, the Skyline Trail is very well-maintained and partly paved, and provides a close-up view of the Nisqually Glacier and an unmatched panoramic view at its apex.

Start: Skyline Trailhead
Distance: 5.5-mile loop
Hiking time: 3–4 hours
Trail surface: Well-maintained; paved and dirt trail in subalpine meadow to rocky alpine trail
Elevation gain: 1,700 feet
Best season: Mid-July through Sept
Nearest towns: Ashford or Packwood

Fees and permits: Vehicle or individual entry fee (7 days); annual entry available; timed entry applies
Trail contacts: Henry M. Jackson Memorial Visitor Center at Paradise, (360) 569-6571
Special considerations: Parking at the Paradise Complex can be a real headache. Come mid-week or off-season for the best chance of finding a spot.

Finding the trailhead: From the Nisqually Entrance Station, travel 16 miles east on Longmire-Paradise Road. Stay to the left (north) where the road forks, following the signs to Paradise. From the Stevens Canyon Entrance Station, travel nearly 19 miles on Stevens Canyon Road to the intersection with Longmire-Paradise Road. Turn right (north) and follow the signs to Paradise. Make your first left into the lower parking lot, which is designated for more than two-hour stays. Walk along the sidewalk toward the upper parking lot and the Henry M. Jackson Memorial Visitor Center. The trail begins directly behind the visitor center. **GPS:** N46 47.183' / W121 44.188'

The Hike

For good reason, more people visit Paradise than any other location on Mount Rainier. The views are spectacular, the services plentiful, and the trails many. Of all the trails in Paradise, Skyline is the most well-known and frequently hiked. As you might guess by the name, the Skyline Trail extends above timberline into alpine terrain, with an awe-inspiring look at the Nisqually Glacier.

For the longest and best view of Mount Rainier, hike this trail clockwise. Start from the Skyline Trailhead by climbing the stairs directly behind the Henry M. Jackson Memorial Visitor Center. Rather than turning right (east), continue straight ahead (north), heading directly up the mountain. With so many intersecting trails, this area can get a bit confusing, but the National Park Service has done a good job of putting up and maintaining clear, direct signposts that explicitly point the way. Stay on the Skyline Trail through all the intersections. You will likely see deer and marmots on this hike. Please do not feed the wildlife. They have already grown bold from constant handouts.

The trail ascends rather steeply for the next 2 miles, so prepare for a workout. At 1.1 miles, the Glacier Vista Trail intersects the main trail. For a slightly closer view of the Nisqually Glacier and a few words on the wonders of glaciation, take the Glacier Vista Trail to your left (west). It parallels the Skyline Trail briefly and then rejoins it. Back on the main trail, continue north for 0.5 mile of switchbacks, at which point the trail splits, the Skyline Trail turning to the right (east) toward Panorama Point, and a spur trail veering to the left (northeast), later connecting with the High Skyline Trail. For a more remarkable view of the mountain, you may wish to take this spur trail, as rocky alpine terrain provides the perfect foreground for a nicely framed Mount Rainier. If you take this trail, however, you miss out on Panorama Point, which is an enjoyable way to learn the topography in the area. Therefore, we recommend staying on the Skyline Trail until you reach Panorama Point, where the National Park Service has erected a panoramic picture of the Tatoosh Range and other mountains in the area with each peak labeled with name and elevation.

Once you have memorized the peaks, continue north on the High Skyline Trail along Pebble Creek. Although you may be tempted to take the Low Skyline Trail, which heads due east, this trail, though lower in elevation, accumulates and retains greater snowpack, rendering it more hazardous and less enjoyable than the High Skyline Trail. Press forward along Pebble Creek Trail until you reach the top of your ascent, where the High Skyline Trail turns right (east). The path straight ahead leads many mountaineers to the base-camp before their summit. You may wish to get a better view of the lines of mountaineers ascending the Muir Snowfield by taking a quick jog up the hill.

Otherwise stay to the right (east), following the High Skyline Trail. You descend steeply along switchbacks in alpine terrain almost all the way to the Golden Gate Trail junction, about 1 mile. The Golden Gate Trail provides a shortcut back to Paradise, cutting about 1.5 miles off the hike length. To stay on the Skyline Trail, bear left.

In 0.6 mile a unique bench made of stone serves as a monument to P. B. Van Trump and Hazard Stevens, for the first recorded successful ascent of Mount Rainier. It also serves as a marker for the trailhead to the Paradise Glacier. Sit and relax on the stone slabs before continuing south on

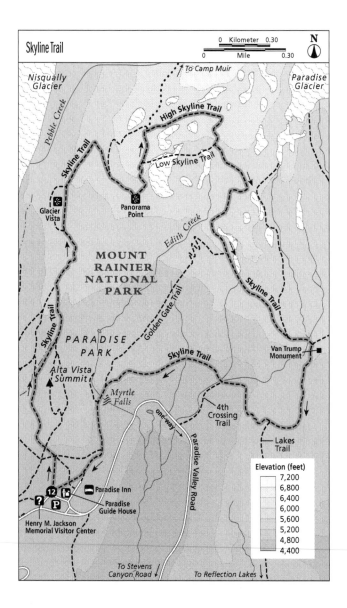

Skyline Trail

To Camp Muir

Nisqually Glacier

Paradise Glacier

Pebble Creek

High Skyline Trail

Low Skyline Trail

Skyline Trail

Glacier Vista

Panorama Point

MOUNT RAINIER NATIONAL PARK

Edith Creek

Skyline Trail

Skyline Trail

Golden Gate Trail

PARADISE PARK

Alta Vista Summit

Van Trump Monument

Myrtle Falls

Skyline Trail

one-way

4th Crossing Trail

Lakes Trail

Paradise Valley Road

Paradise Inn

Paradise Guide House

Henry M. Jackson Memorial Visitor Center

To Stevens Canyon Road

To Reflection Lakes

0   Kilometer   0.30
0   Mile   0.30

N

Elevation (feet)

7,200
6,800
6,400
6,000
5,600
5,200
4,800
4,400

the Skyline Trail. Behind the monument, facing south, you have an excellent view of the Tatoosh Range on a sunny day.

Another 1.4 miles of descent with sporadic switchbacks lead to Myrtle Falls, a pretty little waterfall. You must walk to the bottom of the spur trail, a short side trip, to see it well. Return to the now-paved main trail. You should be able to see Paradise from the trail. Walk 0.5 mile back to the trailhead.

Miles and Directions

0.0 Start from the Skyline Trailhead in the northwestern corner of the Paradise area parking lot. Stay to the left (northwest), heading directly up the mountain.

1.1 The Glacier Vista Trail joins the main Skyline Trail here, then rejoins just up the trail. Take this trail to see the display the park has erected on glaciation.

1.7 A spur trail bypasses Panorama Point on its way to connect to the High Skyline Trail. If the day is clear, stay on the Skyline Trail to the right (southeast) and check out the vista at Panorama Point. Otherwise, go left (northeast) toward more alpine terrain.

2.1 Reach the top of your ascent. Stay on the High Skyline Trail, which converges with the Low Skyline Trail in 0.3 mile.

3.0 Reach the intersection with the Golden Gate Trail. Unless you are in a time crunch, stay to the left (southeast) and remain on the Skyline Trail. If you need to shave 1.5 miles off the hike, you can take the Golden Gate Trail back to Paradise.

3.6 Come to the Paradise Glacier Trail junction and, just beyond it, a surreal rock loveseat in the trail known as the Van Trump Monument. Stay to the right (south) along the Skyline Trail.

5.0 Where the Golden Gate Trail rejoins the Skyline trail on your right, there is also a spur trail to Myrtle Falls on your left. Take this short jog on your left (south) for a quick look at the falls.

5.5 Welcome back to Paradise.

13 Narada Falls

A short jaunt down to the largest falls accessible by car in the park, Narada Falls makes for a worthy side-trip on a cloudy day.

Start: Narada Falls Trailhead
Distance: 0.2 mile out and back
Hiking time: 30 minutes
Trail surface: Well-maintained; soft forest floor and slippery rock
Elevation loss: Minimal
Best season: Early July through Sept
Nearest town: Ashford

Fees and permits: Vehicle or individual entry fee (7 days); annual entry available; timed entry applies
Trail contacts: Henry M. Jackson Memorial Visitor Center at Paradise, (360) 569-6571; Longmire Wilderness Information Center, (360) 569-6650

Finding the trailhead: From the Nisqually Entrance Station, drive approximately 17 miles east on Longmire-Paradise Road; turn right (east) into the parking lot signed for Narada Falls. The Narada Falls Trail is on the far east side of the parking lot, before the restrooms on the right (south). **GPS:** N46 46.512' / W121 44.762'

Options: If you have two vehicles and want a longer downhill, deposit a car at the Longmire Historic District (**GPS:** N46 45.013' / W121 48.750') or Cougar Rock Campground (**GPS:** N46 45.990' / W121 47.464') and walk there from the Narada Falls Trailhead. That way, you experience a less-traveled portion of the Wonderland Trail and pass by three waterfalls—Narada, Madcap and Carter Falls— before crossing the Nisqually River basin. This option would have you descend 2.8 miles (Cougar Rock) or 4.5 miles (Longmire).

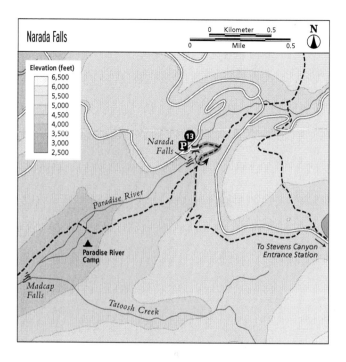

Narada Falls

Elevation (feet)
6,500
6,000
5,500
5,000
4,500
4,000
3,500
3,000
2,500

Narada Falls

Paradise River

Paradise River Camp

Madcap Falls

Tatoosh Creek

To Stevens Canyon Entrance Station

0   Kilometer   0.5

0   Mile   0.5

N

The Hike

From the Narada Falls parking lot, head toward the comfort station. Cross the stone bridge over the Paradise River, which was designed and built employing the naturalistic style that dominated the early 1900s. Find the stone staircase that descends to the right (southeast) toward the falls. A popular waypoint, the area is both well-marked and well-maintained. Follow the trail, turning around one switchback to the foot of Narada Falls. Mist and splash from the cascading water spray the walkway and make for a slippery surface. The park has built a wooden barrier to keep sightseers from getting dangerously close. Mind the barrier and your step as you take in the beauty of the falls. An informational sign instructs on the geological origins of the falls and the andesite ledge over which it tumbles, and the snowfield source of Paradise River's clear waters.

Miles and Directions

0.0 Start at the Narada Falls Trailhead.

0.1 Find yourself at the foot of Narada Falls; read the informative sign and watch your step on the way back.

0.2 Arrive back at the trailhead.

14 Snow Lake

Perfect for children, this short day hike passes one lake and ends at a lake in a glacial cirque nestled at the foot of Unicorn Peak.

Start: Snow Lake Trailhead
Distance: 2.6 miles out and back
Hiking time: 1.5–2.5 hours
Trail surface: Well-maintained; forest and mountain meadow
Elevation gain: 700 feet
Best season: Mid-July through Sept

Nearest towns: Ashford or Packwood
Fees and permits: Vehicle or individual entry fee (7 days); annual entry available; timed entry applies
Trail contacts: Henry M. Jackson Memorial Visitor Center at Paradise, (360) 569-6571

Finding the trailhead: From the Stevens Canyon Entrance Station, drive 16.4 miles west along the winding Stevens Canyon Road. A small parking lot on the left (south) marks the trailhead to Snow Lake. From the Nisqually Entrance Station, travel nearly 16 miles east on Longmire-Paradise Road to the turnoff for the Ohanapecosh area. Turn right (southeast) onto Stevens Canyon Road and toward Ohanapecosh; follow this road for 3 miles total—1.5 miles beyond Reflection Lakes—to the trailhead on your right (south). **GPS:** N46 46.068' / W121 42.466'

The Hike

Trees and brush obscure the Snow Lake Trailhead. When ready to hike, walk to the eastern corner of the parking lot to find the trail, heading south. The trail immediately begins to ascend rather steeply, but do not worry, it eventually levels off and descends, then crosses several ridges throughout the hike.

The trail leads 0.7 mile through subalpine forest to the junction with the path to Bench Lake on the left (east). The path down to the lake is steep, but the bank is worth the struggle, particularly if you fish. Though Bench Lake is cursed by the evasive fish common throughout Mount Rainier, they do rise here, so you may want to pack that pole. Fishing permits are not required, and there are no limits on fish caught. Of course you may not fish for protected species such as bull trout, Dolly Varden, and chinook or coastal cutthroat. Always check the National Park Service website for information on fishing in the park.

Returning to the main trail, you only have 0.5 mile of hiking before you reach Snow Lake, possibly so named because snow once plunged into the lake year-round. In recent years, the snow has melted in late-summer. Always check the trail conditions prior to departure.

When you arrive at the mountain meadow, turn around. This area offers a beautiful view of Mount Rainier. And in the foreground, depending on the season, you can spy a variety of flowers, from glacier lilies to mountain bog gentian, bear grass, huckleberry bushes, and mountain ash.

The last 0.2 mile of trail slopes upward until you see the lovely tarn. The aqua waters of Snow Lake rest in a glacial cirque, and the ancient peaks of the Tatoosh Range rise above it, as glacial runoff cascades down their flanks.

If you have a permit to camp here or simply wish to see the marvelous view from the campsites, turn left (east) at the fork in the trail—a sign points the way. Descend for less than 0.2 mile until the trail crosses a stream out of Snow

Lake. To cross this stream you must traverse a log jam, but in recent years the National Park Service has placed a footbridge over the hazard. As soon as you cross the stream, you reach Snow Lake Camp. The toilet is almost immediately to your left; the campsites are farther down (southeast) and along the lakeside. Site 1 sits on a small peninsula with a view of Unicorn Peak across the aqua waters. A jutting rock makes for a great place to jump in the freezing waters for a refreshing dunk or a painful swim. If you decide to stay at this idyllic spot, be sure to hang your food; black bears have been spotted here.

Please stay off the fragile meadow around Snow Lake and along the trail to the lake. The popularity of this special hike means that each hiker must make special effort to ensure they preserve these meadows for the next person. If you hike this trail, plan to spend some time at the lake; it is lovely. When you're ready to return, just retrace your steps.

Miles and Directions

0.0 Start by walking to the eastern corner of the Snow Lake Trailhead parking lot to find the trail heading south.

0.7 A short trail heads to Bench Lake. If you want to see the lake or fish for a while, take the trail to the left (east). Otherwise, stay on the main trail to Snow Lake.

1.2 As the aqua waters of Snow Lake appear through the trees, you come to the intersection with the Snow Lake Camp trail. We recommend you take the trail to the camp, turning left (east).

1.3 After crossing the log jam, arrive at Snow Lake Camp. Retrace your steps.

2.6 Arrive back at the trailhead.

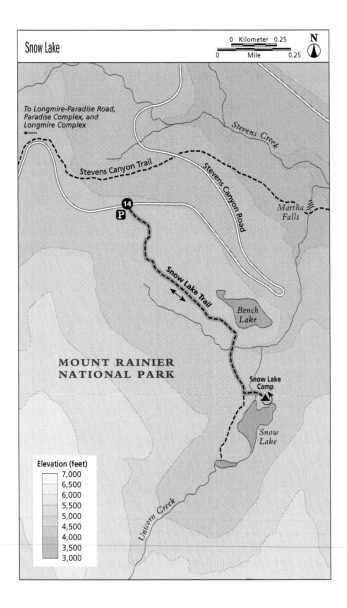

Snow Lake

0 Kilometer 0.25
0 Mile 0.25

N

To Longmire-Paradise Road,
Paradise Complex, and
Longmire Complex

Stevens Creek

Stevens Canyon Trail

Stevens Canyon Road

Martha
Falls

14
P

Snow Lake Trail

Bench
Lake

MOUNT RAINIER
NATIONAL PARK

Snow Lake
Camp

Snow
Lake

Unicorn Creek

Elevation (feet)
7,000
6,500
6,000
5,500
5,000
4,500
4,000
3,500
3,000

Option: Instead of turning left (east) toward Snow Lake Camp, you may choose to follow the path to the right (southwest) at the fork before the lake. This path is 0.3 mile and ends in a small lake-access point. Although the best view of the tarn and Unicorn Peak is at the wilderness camp, the spur trail to the west side of Snow Lake is worth exploring as well. This option adds 0.6 mile total to the trip.

15 Stevens Creek

A one-hour hike in the southern section of the park leads to two unnamed waterfalls swirling among contoured, carved granite.

Start: Box Canyon Picnic Area
Distance: 1.4 miles out and back
Hiking time: 1 hour
Trail surface: Well-maintained; forest
Elevation gain: Minimal
Best season: Late May through Sept
Nearest towns: Ashford or Packwood

Fees and permits: Vehicle or individual entry fee (7 days); annual entry available; timed entry applies
Trail contacts: Henry M. Jackson Memorial Visitor Center at Paradise, (360) 569-6571; Ohanapecosh Visitor Center, (360) 569-6581

Finding the trailhead: From the Stevens Canyon Entrance Station, drive 10.8 miles west on Stevens Canyon Road to the Box Canyon Picnic Area on the left, about 0.3 mile beyond the Box Canyon wayside exhibit. From the Nisqually Entrance Station, travel nearly 16 miles east on Longmire-Paradise Road to the turnoff for the Ohanapecosh area. Turn right (southeast) onto Stevens Canyon Road and toward Ohanapecosh. Stay on this road for 8.6 miles until you reach the Box Canyon Picnic Area. The hike heads south from the picnic area. **GPS:** N46 45.598' / W121 38.362'

The Hike

This trail descends rather steeply through woods full of wildlife to reach two unnamed falls. Well-marked and well-maintained, the trail is easy to follow. The first point of

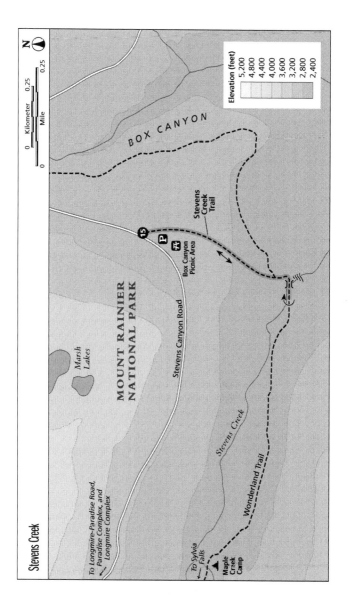

Stevens Creek

MOUNT RAINIER
NATIONAL PARK

Marsh
Lakes

To Longmire-Paradise Road,
Paradise Complex, and
Longmire Complex

Stevens Canyon Road

BOX CANYON

Box Canyon
Picnic Area

Stevens
Creek
Trail

Stevens Creek

Wonderland Trail

To Sylvia
Falls

Maple
Creek
Camp

N

0   Kilometer   0.25

0   Mile

Elevation (feet)
5,200
4,800
4,400
4,000
3,600
3,200
2,800
2,400

interest comes after only 0.5 mile. A sign marks the river viewpoint to your right (west). Only a few paces more and you stand in a fenced clearing, admiring the first waterfall.

Return to the main trail and head right (south) to see the other nameless falls. Walk 0.1 mile beyond the river viewpoint, a total of 0.6 mile from the trailhead, to a junction with the famed Wonderland Trail. Stay to the right (southwest) for 0.1 mile more to reach the bridge over Stevens Creek.

This bridge marks an incredible meeting of stream and stone. Iceberg white water rushing from the glaciers above has rounded these boulders and shaped them into something out of a fairy tale.

When you have appreciated the falls to your content, turn around and follow the same path back to the picnic area. The returning trail is not long, but it is a rather steep ascent; do not be surprised if you are winded by the end.

Miles and Directions

0.0   Start heading south from the Box Canyon Picnic Area.

0.5   A sign points to a vista overlooking an unnamed waterfall. Check out the falls, then continue southwest on the main trail to the intersection with the Wonderland Trail.

0.6   At the junction with the Wonderland Trail, turn right (west) onto the Wonderland Trail.

0.7   Just after you get onto the Wonderland Trail, come to the Stevens Creek crossing. The bridge offers a great look at the multicolored boulders carved and smoothed by the waters of Stevens Creek. Enjoy the view before retracing your steps.

1.4   Arrive back at the trailhead.

16 Box Canyon

This very short loop crosses a bridge over a deep, narrow gorge carved by the erosive action of a silt-laden river.

Start: Box Canyon wayside exhibit
Distance: 0.3-mile loop
Hiking time: 30 minutes
Trail surface: Well-maintained; mostly paved
Elevation gain: Minimal
Best season: May through Sept
Nearest towns: Ashford or Packwood

Fees and permits: Vehicle or individual entry fee (7 days); annual entry available; timed entry applies
Trail contacts: Henry M. Jackson Memorial Visitor Center at Paradise, (360) 569-6571; Ohanapecosh Visitor Center, (360) 569-6581

Finding the trailhead: From the Stevens Canyon Entrance Station, drive 10.5 miles west on Stevens Canyon Road to the Box Canyon wayside exhibit. Parking is on the left (south). If you pass the Box Canyon Picnic Area, you have gone 0.3 mile too far west. From the Nisqually Entrance Station, travel nearly 16 miles east on Longmire-Paradise Road to the turnoff for the Ohanapecosh area. Turn right (southeast) onto Stevens Canyon Road and toward Ohanapecosh. Stay on this road for 9 miles until you reach the Box Canyon wayside exhibit, 0.3 mile past the Box Canyon Picnic Area. The paved trail begins across the street from the parking lot to the right (east) of the bridge. **GPS:** N46 45.950' / W121 38.115'

The Hike

This hike is great for those interested in glaciers and glacial rivers. The Box Canyon Trail showcases the powerful polishing force of a glacier and the effects of long-term erosion by its silt-filled water. The paved trail takes you past

Box Canyon

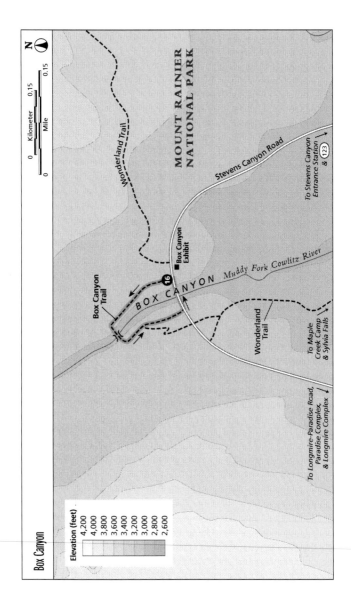

Elevation (feet)
- 4,200
- 4,000
- 3,800
- 3,600
- 3,400
- 3,200
- 3,000
- 2,800
- 2,600

Wonderland Trail

MOUNT RAINIER NATIONAL PARK

Stevens Canyon Road

Box Canyon Exhibit

To Stevens Canyon Entrance Station & 123

Box Canyon Trail

BOX CANYON *Muddy Fork Cowlitz River*

16

Wonderland Trail

To Maple Creek Camp & Sylvia Falls

To Longmire-Paradise Road, Paradise Complex, & Longmire Complex

N

0   Kilometer   0.15

0   Mile   0.15

wildflowers and into a thundering canyon. For the first half of this hike, the paved trail is wide, smooth, and wheelchair accessible. The entire hike is paved, but the second stretch is considerably rougher and would prove tumultuous travel for a wheelchair.

At the trailhead there is an informational sign about the hike. After reading it, head straight up the trail. The trail merging from the right (northeast) is the Wonderland Trail. Notice the bare rocks on the right side of the canyon, where a powerful glacier once polished the surface.

A little more than 0.1 mile into your hike is a bridge over Muddy Fork. Take the time to look down and enjoy the unique canyon. After you cross the bridge, the trail is paved, but less maintained, all the way to where it rejoins Stevens Canyon Road. Either retrace your steps or walk along the road to loop back to your car.

Miles and Directions

0.0   Head north across the Stevens Canyon Road from the Box Canyon exhibit to the Box Canyon Trail, a short informative section of the Wonderland Trail.

0.1   At the bridge crossing the Muddy Fork of the Cowlitz River, continue across the bridge to the other side of the loop.

0.2   The Wonderland Trail splits off on its route around Mount Rainier. Stay to the left (southeast) back to the Box Canyon exhibit.

0.3   Skirt the Stevens Canyon Road to arrive back at the trailhead.

17 Silver Falls

This beautiful, wooded day hike originating near the Ohanapecosh Visitor Center is a popular trail for campers, who can reach a spectacular waterfall from the convenience of their campsites.

Start: Silver Falls Loop Trailhead/ Ohanapecosh Visitor Center
Distance: 2.7-mile loop
Hiking time: 1.5–2 hours
Trail surface: Well-maintained; soft forest floor
Elevation gain: Minimal
Best season: May through Sept

Nearest town: Packwood
Fees and permits: Vehicle or individual entry fee (7 days); annual entry available; no timed entry required
Trail contacts: Ohanapecosh Visitor Center, (360) 569-6581

Finding the trailhead: From Packwood drive 7 miles northeast on US 12 to the junction with WA 123. Turn left (north) onto WA 123 and continue for 3 miles to the turnoff for Ohanapecosh Campground, just 1.8 miles south of the Stevens Canyon Entrance Station. Turn left (west) and immediately right again at the fork in the road toward the campground. Continue on this road as it winds past the visitor center. Go right (north) toward the day parking area. Loop around to enter the parking lot from the other (east) side. On the way you will see the Silver Falls Trailhead to your left (north). Park and walk to the trailhead. **GPS:** N46 44.210' / W121 33.888'

The Hike

Silver Falls opens early in the year due to its low elevation, and visitors can enjoy the falls as early as May. The trail wanders through a beautiful forest. Traffic can be very heavy on this trail, since the trailhead is located at Ohanapecosh Campground.

The first 0.1 mile of this hike is also part of an educational self-guided loop trail that explains the Mount Rainier ecosystem. Stay left (north) when the Hot Springs Trail forks off to the right.

The beginning of the trail runs through a thermal area. You will see hot springs and interpretive signs telling you more about the thermal features. The ground is fragile and easily damaged here, making it especially important that you stay on the trail. Walking off the trail in this area is illegal, and park officials may cite violators. Remember that water originating from hot springs is unsafe for human consumption.

The trail gains a bit of elevation in the beginning. You will cross two bridges before you reach the bridge over Laughingwater Creek. Both of these bridges cross streams that empty into the Ohanapecosh River, which is to your left (west). At 0.9 mile you reach Laughingwater Creek, aptly named as the water bounces and frolics over the rocks. Cross Laughingwater Creek and walk 0.2 mile to the Laughingwater Trail junction. Stay to the left and on the Silver Falls Loop.

Silver Falls is 0.1 mile from the Laughingwater Trail junction, 1.2 miles into your hike. An overlook, 0.1 mile from where you first see the falls, faces the shining waters of Silver Falls. Take your time and enjoy the marvelous view until you are ready to move on. We must emphasize that the rocks at Silver Falls are moss covered and slippery. People have lost their lives as a result of disregarding the warning signs posted by the falls. Please stay behind the guardrails.

The second half of the loop, though slightly longer, is not as eventful as the first half, but the trail winds through a

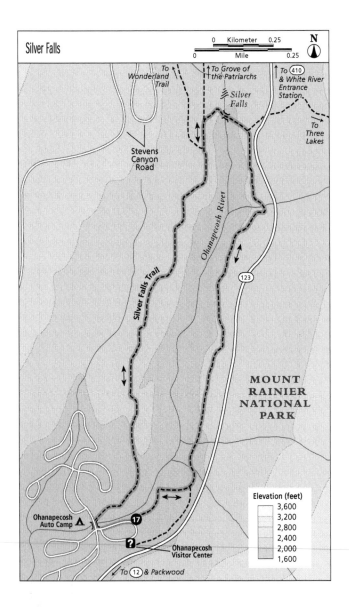

Silver Falls

Kilometer
0   0.25

Mile
0   0.25

N

To Wonderland Trail

To Grove of the Patriarchs

Silver Falls

To 410 & White River Entrance Station

To Three Lakes

Stevens Canyon Road

Ohanapecosh River

Silver Falls Trail

123

MOUNT RAINIER NATIONAL PARK

Ohanapecosh Auto Camp

17

Ohanapecosh Visitor Center

To 12 & Packwood

Elevation (feet)

3,600
3,200
2,800
2,400
2,000
1,600

pleasant mixture of western hemlock, Douglas fir, and western red cedar. The trail exits at a different location within the campground from where it began; simply walk over the bridge and head back to the day parking lot.

Miles and Directions

0.0 Start at the trailhead near the Ohanapecosh Visitor Center.

0.1 Hot Springs Trail forks to the right; stay to the left (north) on the Silver Falls Trail.

1.1 At the Laughingwater Trail junction, stay to the left (north). Again, head toward Silver Falls.

1.2 Enjoy Silver Falls, but stay behind the barricades.

1.4 Just 0.2 mile beyond Silver Falls and the Silver Falls overlook, reach the Eastside Trail. Take a sharp left (south), heading back toward the Ohanapecosh Visitor Center and Campground.

1.5 Stay to the left (south) at the Cowlitz Divide Trail junction.

2.7 The end of the loop drops you off at the Ohanapecosh Campground, just north of the road you came in on and across the Ohanapecosh River from the parking lot.

18   Grove of the Patriarchs

This short interpretive hike crosses the Ohanapecosh River by way of suspension bridge and takes you to a magnificent old-growth forest with thousand-year-old trees.

Start: Grove of the Patriarchs parking lot
Distance: 1.1-mile lollipop
Hiking time: 1 hour
Trail surface: Well-maintained; forest
Elevation gain: Minimal
Best season: May through Sept

Nearest town: Packwood
Fees and permits: Vehicle or individual entry fee (7 days); annual entry available; timed entry applies
Trail contacts: Ohanapecosh Visitor Center, (360) 569-6581

Finding the trailhead: From Stevens Canyon Entrance Station, go west 0.2 mile on Stevens Canyon Road to a parking lot on your right (north), marked by a sign that reads Grove of the Patriarchs. The trailhead is to the right (south) of the restrooms. **GPS:** N46 45.496' / W121 33.440'

The Hike

The trail is very well-maintained but often muddy, due to its low elevation and proximity to the Ohanapecosh River. Wear appropriate foot gear and remember to step through the mud instead of around it to avoid widening the trails. Interpretive signs line the trail, helping you discern differences between the western hemlock, Douglas fir, and western red cedar. This is a great trail to take if you are interested in learning more about the life cycles and species of old-growth forests.

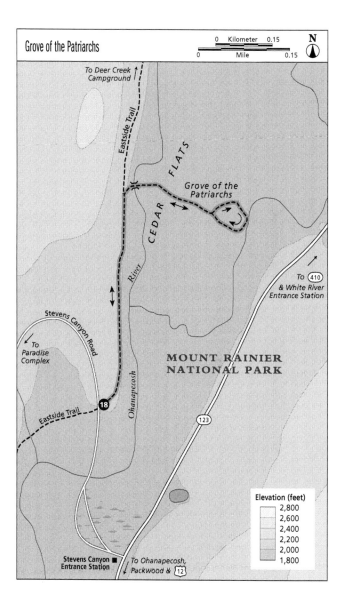

Grove of the Patriarchs

0   Kilometer   0.15

0   Mile   0.15

N

To Deer Creek
Campground

Eastside Trail

CEDAR FLATS

Grove of the
Patriarchs

River

To (410)
& White River
Entrance Station

Stevens Canyon Road

To
Paradise
Complex

MOUNT RAINIER
NATIONAL PARK

Ohanapecosh

18

Eastside Trail

(123)

Stevens Canyon
Entrance Station

To Ohanapecosh,
Packwood & (12)

Elevation (feet)

2,800
2,600
2,400
2,200
2,000
1,800

The Ohanapecosh River flows on your right for the first 0.3 mile as the trail meanders through old-growth forest. The waters run unusually clear for a glacial river; the inactivity of the Ohanapecosh Glacier reduces the amount of suspended glacial flour.

The trail forks 0.3 mile into the hike. The Eastside Trail continues heading north; the Grove of the Patriarchs Trail veers off to the right (east) toward a bridge over the Ohanapecosh River. In 2021, the suspension bridge suffered heavy damage as a result of flooding, requiring replacement. The new bridge links to an island rich with old-growth forest. Some of the towering firs and cedars register at more than 1,000 years old.

Around 0.1 mile past the Grove of the Patriarchs junction, the trail splits to form a loop. The loop section of the trail consists of a wooden boardwalk; please protect the trees and other plants on the forest floor by staying on the boardwalk. Go left (northeast) around the loop. Make sure to check out the humbling height and circumference of the red cedar about halfway through the loop. Continue along the loop until you are back to the stem of the lollipop. The return trip gives you a chance to apply your newfound tree identification skills.

Miles and Directions

0.0 Follow the signs to the Grove of the Patriarchs and the Eastside Trail, heading east on the right of the restrooms. The trail quickly turns north to parallel the crystal clear Ohanapecosh River.

0.3 The Grove of the Patriarchs Trail splinters off the Eastside Trail to cross the Ohanapecosh River.

0.4 The stem of the lollipop trail splits in two; we recommend going left around this loop section.

1.1 Return the way you came to arrive back at the parking lot.

19 Naches Peak

A popular loop for photographers, Naches Peak Trail circles small mountain lakes through subalpine forest with striking images of Mount Rainier in the distance.

Start: Naches Peak Trailhead
Distance: 5.0-mile loop
Hiking time: 2–3 hours
Trail surface: Well-maintained; subalpine forest
Elevation gain: Minimal
Best season: Late July through Oct

Nearest town: Greenwater
Fees and permits: Possible fee for use of the national forest (Dewey Lake); no timed entry required
Trail contacts: White River Wilderness Information Center, (360) 569-6670

Finding the trailhead: From the junction of WA 410 and WA 123 on the eastern edge of the park, drive east on WA 410 to Chinook Pass. Continue east, out of the park, and park in the Tipsoo Lake parking lot on the right (south) side of the road just west of Chinook Pass. Walk west along the highway for less than 0.5 mile to the large park entrance sign above the road. The top of the sign doubles as a bridge; the trailhead sign is on the north side of the bridge. **GPS:** N46 52.335' / W121 30.935'

The Hike

The Naches Peak Trail straddles the national park boundary, which means two things: first, you do not have to pay an entrance fee to hike this trail; second, pets are allowed on the portion of the trail outside the park boundary. These facts, coupled with a nice picnic area and stellar views, make

Naches Peak a popular summer hike. The vibrant fall colors bring visitors in the autumn.

The first 2 miles of trail are outside the park and along the Pacific Crest Trail. Because this part of the Naches Peak Loop is pet friendly, you may see many hikers with leashed dogs and the occasional horseback rider. If you bring a pet, however, you cannot complete the loop and must turn around at the park entrance signs where the Naches Peak Trail intersects the Pacific Crest Trail.

From the Naches Peak Trailhead, cross the bridge to the southeast side of WA 410. The trail ascends steadily, passing a few small subalpine lakes. Trails lead to the lakes, but they are not maintained, and trekking through such fragile meadow is discouraged. Stay on the trail.

The trail reaches its highest point just before entering the park and quickly curves eastward. Soon, 2.2 miles into the hike, the Pacific Crest Trail branches left (south) toward Dewey Lake; the Naches Peak Loop continues straight ahead (west).

Continuing along the Naches Peak Trail, you round the bend to catch a great view of Mount Rainier. In fact, this part of the hike boasts some of the most spectacular views of the entire eastern slope. If you have a topographical map, you can try to identify Little Tahoma, the Cowlitz Chimneys, Governors Ridge, and Seymour Peak to the west.

The trail wraps to the right, around Naches Peak. Wildflowers blanket the meadows in midsummer; huckleberries do the same in late summer. The trail also passes a small mountain lake on this side of the peak. As the trail turns north, you can see Tipsoo Lake, with its parking lot and picnic tables.

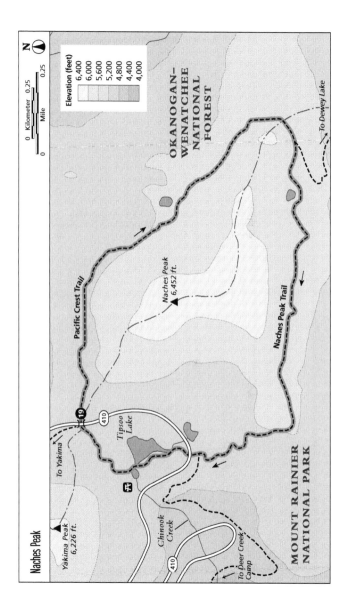

Naches Peak

N

0 Kilometer 0.25
0 Mile 0.25

Elevation (feet)
6,400
6,000
5,600
5,200
4,800
4,400
4,000

OKANOGAN–
WENATCHEE
NATIONAL
FOREST

To Dewey Lake

Pacific Crest Trail

Naches Peak
6,452 ft.

Naches Peak Trail

To Yakima

410

19

Tipsoo
Lake

Yakima Peak
6,226 ft.

Chinook Creek

410

To Deer Creek Camp

MOUNT RAINIER
NATIONAL PARK

To reach the picnic area, 4.6 miles into the hike, you must cross WA 410. The continuing trail is visible across the road. A maintained trail loops around Tipsoo Lake, if you are up for a casual stroll.

The steepest incline on the hike is left for the end. The trail passes just north of the picnic area, switches back a few times, then sets you back at the trailhead. Walk east along WA 410 to return to your car.

Miles and Directions

0.0 Start heading east on the Pacific Crest Trail/Naches Peak Trail on the path that goes over the Mount Rainier National Park entrance sign that straddles WA 410 at the park boundary.

2.2 Almost halfway through the loop, the Pacific Crest Trail spurs off to the left (south) and heads toward Dewey Lake.

4.6 Reach WA 410; the trail continues on the other side.

4.7 Arrive at the banks of Tipsoo Lake just after crossing the road.

5.0 After skirting the lake and climbing in forest, you have come full circle back to the trailhead on WA 410.

20 Silver Forest

Enjoy an easy one-hour walk to informative viewpoints along a flowery subalpine meadow.

Start: Sunrise Complex
Distance: 2.0 miles out and back
Hiking time: 1 hour
Trail surface: Well-maintained; dirt trail and subalpine meadow
Elevation gain: Minimal
Best season: Mid-July through Sept

Nearest town: Greenwater
Fees and permits: Vehicle or individual entry fee (7 days); annual entry available; timed entry applies
Trail contacts: White River Wilderness Information Center, (360) 569-6670; Sunrise Visitor Center, (360) 663-2425

Finding the trailhead: From the White River Entrance Station, drive 13.8 miles west on White River Road to the Sunrise Complex parking lot. Park in one of the many spaces provided. The trailhead is south of the parking lot. **GPS:** N46 54.842' / W121 38.516'

The Hike

The Silver Forest Trail involves two parts. First, a short descent leads to two informative exhibits with great views of Mount Rainier. Then the trail continues east through subalpine forest and meadow.

To find the trailhead, park in the Sunrise parking lot. From the south side of the lot, directly across from the ranger station and cafeteria, a trail heads south and a dirt road heads west. As the sign directs, follow the southbound trail, the Emmons Vista Nature Trail.

In only 0.1 mile you reach the junction with the Sunrise Rim Trail. Stay to the left (south). The path curves east, and a sign points south to the first Emmons Vista exhibit. Walk down to the viewpoint and admire the tree-framed view of the Emmons and Winthrop Glaciers. The exhibit explains the various features of a glaciated mountain and how they were formed.

Return to the main trail and continue east. You soon come upon the second exhibit, again immediately south of the trail. This vista point has a nice, sheltered seating area and two more informative signs. The first, snow shadow, includes climatic information about the winds and snow of Paradise. The other, rocks riding on air, gives a historical account of the Little Tahoma Peak rockslide of 1963.

Back on the main trail, head east once again. In less than 0.1 mile, you come to a sign indicating that you have reached the Silver Forest portion of the trail. A fire of unknown origins incinerated this area long ago. Today the only remnants of the old forest are "silver sentinels," long-dead but standing trees. In the fire's wake, subalpine trees and wildflowers have grown, making this forest particularly intriguing. Small, gnarled trees are dispersed throughout this meadow, along with blankets of wildflowers in midsummer. Walk along this trail for 0.8 mile before reaching a sign that indicates the end of the maintained trail, 1 mile from the trailhead. The trail continues for quite some distance beyond this sign, so venture farther if you want an extended hike. Otherwise, turn around and walk back to the Sunrise Complex.

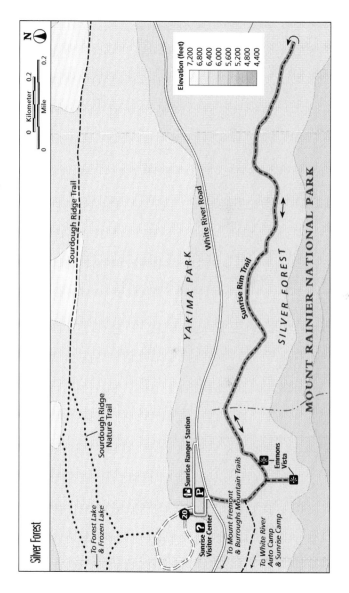

Silver Forest

N

0   Kilometer   0.2
0   Mile   0.2

Elevation (feet)
7,200
6,800
6,400
6,000
5,600
5,200
4,800
4,400

Sourdough Ridge Trail

Sourdough Ridge Nature Trail

To Forest Lake & Frozen Lake

YAKIMA PARK

White River Road

Sunrise Ranger Station

Sunrise Visitor Center

20

To Mount Fremont & Burroughs Mountain Trails

To White River Auto Camp & Sunrise Camp

Emmons Vista

Sunrise Rim Trail

SILVER FOREST

MOUNT RAINIER NATIONAL PARK

Miles and Directions

0.0 Start heading south on the trail across the parking lot from the snack bar and gift shop.

0.1 In just a short while, reach the juncture of the Emmons Vista and Sunrise Rim Trails. Stay to the left (east) toward the Emmons Vista exhibits.

0.2 There are two Emmons Vista exhibits, one with information on glaciation and one on climatic conditions. Both have viewpoints.

1.0 The trail heads through a silver fir forest and peters out. Retrace your steps.

2.0 Arrive back at the trailhead.

21 Emmons Moraine

A short hike up to and along the Emmons Moraine provides an excellent view of the Emmons Glacier, the largest glacier in the contiguous United States.

Start: Glacier Basin Trailhead
Distance: 2.8 miles out and back
Hiking time: 1.5-2.5 hours
Trail surface: Well-maintained; forest floor, rocky river bed, and dusty moraine
Elevation gain: 960 feet
Best season: Early July through Sept

Nearest town: Greenwater
Fees and permits: Vehicle or individual entry fee (7 days); annual entry available; timed entry applies
Trail contacts: White River Wilderness Information Center, (360) 569-6670

Finding the trailhead: From the White River Entrance Station, drive 4 miles west on White River Road to the White River Campground turnoff. Turn left (northwest) toward the campground, and drive another mile to the parking area on the left. A sign indicates that the parking lot is for backpackers and climbers. Park here and walk west to the Glacier Basin Trailhead at the westernmost tip of loop D, the last loop in White River Campground. **GPS:** N46 54.094' / W121 38.763'

The Hike

This short, gradual uphill hike is great for older children and adults looking for a close-up view of the largest glacier in the contiguous forty-eight states. Hike along the Emmons Moraine for an unobstructed view of the Emmons Glacier and its basin, an expansive section of the earth carved out by the glacier in years past.

Head west along the Glacier Basin Trail. Just steps from the trailhead, you come to a billboard with information about old copper mines in the alpine area above the moraine. From here, the hike begins in shaded forest, continues straight, and turns into switchbacks, which offer peeks at an unnamed waterfall at their east end. After less than a mile, you reach the junction with the Emmons Moraine Trail. At the junction go left (southwest), up the Emmons Moraine Trail.

This portion of the trail has become more hazardous over the years, as flooding has carved a creek bed in the moraine, which requires that you walk over a footbridge and along a steep, silted ledge before turning the corner and heading west toward Mount Rainier and the Emmons Glacier. Once you have braved these obstacles, however, the trail along the moraine is rather straight and unobstructed as it climbs upward. But if you look off the trail to your left, you will see that the moraine dives steeply toward the headwaters of the White River. On the trail, your feet sink into the silt deposits left by the Emmons Glacier's advancement. On a hot day, the sand soaks up the sun, adding to the scorching heat, and the small trees along the Emmons Moraine provide little or no shade. Be sure to bring sunscreen.

Little Tahoma Peak and Mount Rainier frame the Emmons Glacier to the west and Baker Point stands to the south. When you have marveled at the Emmons Glacier long enough, head back the same way you came.

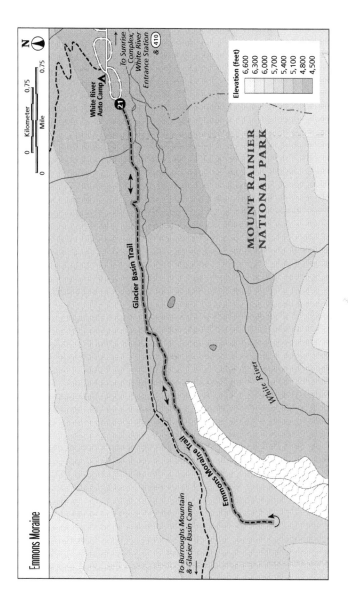

Emmons Moraine

MOUNT RAINIER NATIONAL PARK

White River Auto Camp

To Sunrise Complex, White River Entrance Station & 410

21

Glacier Basin Trail

Emmons Moraine Trail

To Burroughs Mountain & Glacier Basin Camp

White River

N

Kilometer   0   0.75
Mile   0   0.75

Elevation (feet)
6,600
6,300
6,000
5,700
5,400
5,100
4,800
4,500

Miles and Directions

0.0 Start heading west on the Glacier Basin Trail from loop D of the White River Campground.

0.9 Emmons Moraine Trail separates from the Glacier Basin Trail toward the left (southwest); take the Emmons Moraine spur trail.

1.4 Emmons Moraine Trail ends with a view of the glacial wake. Enjoy the view before heading back the way you came.

2.8 Arrive back at the trailhead.

22 Mount Fremont Lookout

This hike makes a short ascent to a fire lookout on Mount Fremont that towers over the north side of the park. The lookout affords great views of Mount Rainier, Skyscraper Mountain, Grand Park, and Sourdough Ridge.

Start: Sunrise Complex
Distance: 5.4 miles out and back
Hiking time: 3–4 hours
Trail surface: Well-maintained; dirt trail and scree field with steep ledges at places
Elevation gain: 781 feet
Best season: Early July through Sept

Nearest town: Greenwater
Fees and permits: Vehicle or individual entry fee (7 days); annual entry available; timed entry applies
Trail contacts: White River Wilderness Information Center, (360) 569-6670; Sunrise Visitor Center, (360) 663-2425

Finding the trailhead: From the White River Entrance Station, drive 13.8 miles west on the White River Road to the Sunrise Complex parking lot. Park and walk to the trailhead on the northwestern end of the lot, to the right of the restrooms. **GPS:** N46 54.948' / W121 38.623'

The Hike

Walk up the paved path to the right (east) of the restrooms until you see a dirt trail on your right (north). Get on that trail and travel north until you come to a fork in the Sourdough Ridge Nature Trail. Turn left (northwest) and walk 0.2 mile to the Sourdough Ridge Trail. Turn left (west) onto the Sourdough Ridge Trail.

While you are walking along this trail, you can see the North Cascades to your right. Mount Rainier also looms magnificent from Sourdough Ridge. After 0.3 mile you pass the Huckleberry Creek Trail on your right, heading northwest. Keep going west (left) another 0.8 mile to a five-way junction, immediately after Frozen Lake and 1.4 miles from the trailhead. At this junction the Mount Fremont Trail is the first trail on your right; follow it, heading north. The trail runs above timberline for the remainder of the hike. Fat marmots inhabit the green meadows along the trail. Keep in mind that it is illegal to feed animals and detrimental to their natural survival skills.

Soon the trail threads along the talus fields of Mount Fremont. Watch your step—the ledge drops straight off the ridge! Low-growing subalpine wildflowers line the trail in late July. Walk along the ridge until you reach the lookout, 2.7 miles from the Sunrise Complex. From the lookout you can see all the way to the north end of the park, where clearcuts begin to shave indiscriminate splotches in the forest. Skyscraper Mountain is to your left, just beyond the deep green and flower fields of Berkeley Park. North of Berkeley Park you can easily identify Grand Park, a massive plateau dappled with ghost trees. Mount Rainier towers above it all. Take the time to get out your map and identify the landmarks around you.

Miles and Directions

0.0   Start from the Sunrise parking lot, and follow the paved path to the right (east) of the restrooms, heading north. Don't let the road heading off to the left (west) tempt you; stay on the main trail, heading north past the informative display.

Mount Fremont Lookout

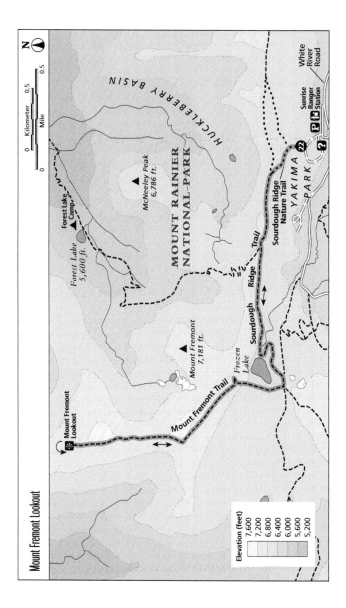

Elevation (feet)
- 7,600
- 7,200
- 6,800
- 6,400
- 6,000
- 5,600
- 5,200

Mount Fremont Lookout

Mount Fremont Trail

Mount Fremont 7,181 ft.

Frozen Lake

Forest Lake Camp

Forest Lake 5,600 ft.

McNeeley Peak 6,786 ft.

MOUNT RAINIER NATIONAL PARK

HUCKLEBERRY BASIN

Sourdough Ridge Trail

Sourdough Ridge Nature Trail

YAKIMA PARK

Sunrise Ranger Station

White River Road

0   Kilometer   0.5

0   Mile   0.5

N

0.1 The Sourdough Ridge Nature Trail forks; stay to the left (northwest) toward Frozen Lake and Mount Fremont.

0.3 Reach the top of Sourdough Ridge and the junction with the Sourdough Ridge Trail. Take a left (west) onto the trail.

0.6 Bypass the steep Huckleberry Creek Trail on your right (north).

1.4 Just beyond Frozen Lake, come to the Mount Fremont Trail junction. Follow the trail to the right (north).

2.7 After more than a mile of uphill along a rocky mountain slope, you reach Mount Fremont Lookout. Enjoy the view, and then retrace your steps.

5.4 Arrive back at the trailhead.

23 Forest Lake

A short descent over rocky alpine terrain travels through sub-alpine meadows to a quaint mountain lake.

Start: Sunrise Complex
Distance: 5.0 miles out and back
Hiking time: 3-4 hours
Trail surface: Well-maintained; forest floor and alpine rocky trail
Elevation gain: 1,200 feet
Best season: Mid-July through Sept

Nearest town: Greenwater
Fees and permits: Vehicle or individual entry fee (7 days); annual entry available; timed entry applies
Trail contacts: White River Wilderness Information Center, (360) 569-6670; Sunrise Visitor Center, (360) 663-2425

Finding the trailhead: From the White River Entrance Station, drive 13.8 miles west on White River Road to the Sunrise Complex parking lot. Park and walk to the trailhead on the north end of the lot, to the right of the restrooms. **GPS:** N46 54.948' / W121 38.623'

The Hike

If you want to escape the crowd at Sunrise and experience a variety of different ecosystems, but do not mind missing out on the best views of Mount Rainier, consider heading to Forest Lake. From the tundra on the north side of Sourdough Ridge to the deciduous forest that surrounds Forest Lake, you will have a taste of everything.

Walk up the paved path to the right (east) of the restrooms until the trail forks. Take the dirt trail on your right (north). Walk up that trail until you come to the junction with the Sourdough Ridge Nature Trail. Turn left (northwest) onto the nature trail and walk 0.2 mile to the Sourdough Ridge Trail. Turn left (west) onto the Sourdough Ridge Trail.

While you are walking along this trail, you can see the Cascades to the north and Mount Rainier to the southwest. Enjoy these views because once you turn off onto the Huckleberry Creek Trail they disappear. At 0.6 mile into your hike, Huckleberry Trail splits off to the right (north); follow it uphill briefly before beginning your long descent to Forest Lake. The first part of the trail is in the alpine zone and relatively rocky. There are low-growing wildflowers, such as red mountain heather, all around. Patches of snow might linger on the trail until August, but the trail is usually easy to follow.

As you descend into the flowery meadows below, keep your eye out for wildlife on both Mount Fremont (on your left) and McNeeley Peak (right). Carved between the two peaks, the lush Huckleberry Basin benefits from their snowmelt. The trail heads into the trees and wanders through forest and meadows, overflowing with wildflowers in late July. If you time it right, you will be treated to innumerable blooms of purple-and-yellow elephant head lousewort all the way to Forest Lake. True to their name, these unusual blooms seem to emulate the wide ears and long trunk of the giant creatures. The lake itself is small but charming. Next to the campsite you'll spot a great place to take a break and enjoy the lake.

Miles and Directions

0.0 Start from the Sunrise parking lot; follow the paved path to the right (east) of the restrooms heading north. Don't let the road heading off to the left (west) tempt you; stay on the main trail, heading north past the informative display.

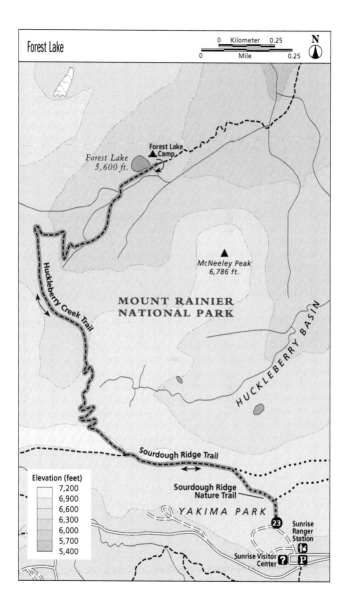

Forest Lake

0 Kilometer 0.25
0 Mile 0.25

N

Forest Lake
5,600 ft.

Forest Lake
Camp

McNeeley Peak
6,786 ft.

Huckleberry Creek Trail

MOUNT RAINIER
NATIONAL PARK

HUCKLEBERRY BASIN

Sourdough Ridge Trail

Elevation (feet)
7,200
6,900
6,600
6,300
6,000
5,700
5,400

Sourdough Ridge
Nature Trail

YAKIMA PARK

23

Sunrise
Ranger
Station

Sunrise Visitor
Center

P

0.1 The Sourdough Ridge Nature Trail forks; stay to the left (northwest) toward Frozen Lake and Mount Fremont.

0.3 Reach the top of Sourdough Ridge and the junction with the Sourdough Ridge Trail. Take a left (west) onto the trail.

0.6 Turn right (north) onto the Huckleberry Creek Trail, heading sharply down the hillside.

2.5 At Forest Lake and the Forest Lake Camp, you have reached your destination. Enjoy! Then head back the way you came.

5.0 Arrive back at the trailhead.

24 Sunrise Rim

This loop travels along Sourdough Ridge, over the first hump of Burroughs Mountain, to an overlook of the Emmons Glacier, and descends along Sunrise Rim, past Shadow Lake, and back to the Sunrise Complex.

Start: Sunrise Complex
Distance: 4.9-mile loop
Hiking time: 2.5–4 hours
Trail surface: Well-maintained; dirt trail, subalpine forest, rocky alpine terrain
Elevation gain: 840 feet
Best season: Aug through Sept
Nearest town: Greenwater

Fees and permits: Vehicle or individual entry fee (7 days); annual entry available; timed entry applies
Trail contacts: White River Wilderness Information Center, (360) 569-6670; Sunrise Visitor Center, (360) 663-2425

Finding the trailhead: From the White River Entrance Station, drive 13.8 miles west on White River Road to the Sunrise Complex parking lot. Park and walk to the trailhead on the north end of the lot, to the right of the restrooms. **GPS:** N46 54.948' / W121 38.623'

The Hike

While exploring the scenic area around the Sunrise Complex, this hike offers rare views of a wide range of landscapes in a relatively short loop. You walk along Sourdough Ridge, climb to the first hump of Burroughs Mountain, and look over the Emmons Glacier. Finally, you descend to Shadow Lake, through subalpine forest and back to the Sunrise parking lot.

Walk up the paved path to the right (east) of the restrooms until you see a dirt trail on your right heading north. Get on the trail and walk until you come to a fork in the Sourdough Ridge Nature Trail. Turn left (northwest) and walk 0.2 mile to the Sourdough Ridge Trail. Turn left (west) onto the Sourdough Ridge Trail.

While you are walking along this trail, you can see the Cascades to your right; on really clear days you can even see Mount Baker. Mount Rainier also looks magnificent from Sourdough Ridge. You will walk a total of 0.3 mile along the ridge, 0.6 mile from the Sunrise Complex, to the Huckleberry Creek Trail on your right, heading northwest. Stay to the left and on the Sourdough Ridge Trail for another 0.8 mile to the junction with Burroughs Mountain Trail. Directly before the junction, you pass Frozen Lake to your right (north). As the signs tell you, Frozen Lake provides a domestic water supply; the National Park Service has fenced in the lake to avoid possible human contamination. The fence is not very aesthetically pleasing, but it is necessary.

Once you have reached the five-trail junction, take the Burroughs Mountain Trail, which heads uphill to the left (southwest). Steep snowfields cover this trail into August in some years. Sturdy boots and an ice ax are recommended. The trail up to the First Burroughs gains about 200 feet and travels through alpine terrain. The vegetation in this area is very fragile and susceptible to human impact. Please stay on the trail to avoid damaging the delicate ecosystem.

From Burroughs Mountain, you can see Old Desolate to the northwest and Berkeley Park to the north. Old Desolate is a barren plateau that sticks out among forested hills. It is quite a contrast to the bright wildflowers that fill Berkeley Park.

When you reach the crest of First Burroughs Mountain, 0.7 mile from Frozen Lake, turn left (east) onto the Sunrise Rim Trail. To the south is the Emmons Glacier, the largest glacier in the contiguous United States. A better view of the glacier comes from the glacier overlook, 1 mile away. It is all downhill to the overlook and to Sunrise Camp.

You can see the entire Emmons Glacier and the beginning of the White River from the glacial overlook. Goat Island Mountain towers above both these natural wonders. The White River originates from the Emmons Glacier and is filled with glacial flour. Notice that there are several pools in the valley below. These pools appear sea-foam green due to the large concentration of sediment suspended in their waters. The sun reflects light off the cloudy waters to produce this gorgeous color. It is amazing to imagine that the Emmons Glacier once filled the valley below.

From the glacial overlook, continue heading downhill to Sunrise Camp until you reach a fork in the trail. Turn right (east) toward Sunrise Camp. To your left, an administrative road heads north and passes Sunrise Camp. Continue going east on the Sunrise Rim Trail.

Just 0.2 mile east of this intersection, a total of 3.6 miles into your hike, Shadow Lake appears to the left. Previous hikers have greatly damaged the area around Shadow Lake, the water source for Sunrise Camp. Again, please stay on the trail to reduce your personal impact on the lake.

The remainder of the loop travels through the subalpine meadows of Yakima Park. In July and early August, Yakima Park is filled with a variety of wildflowers. At times you can see Goat Island Mountain and the Emmons Glacier from the trail. The trail is flat until you intersect the Wonderland Trail,

Sunrise Rim

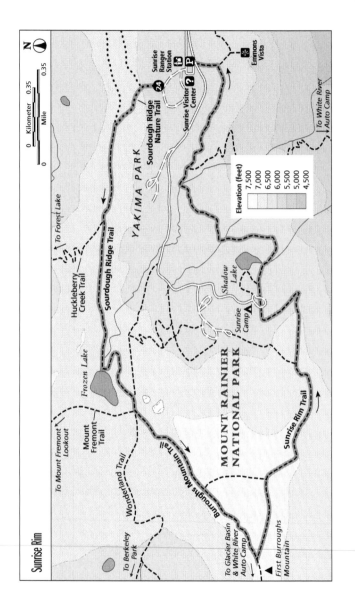

Elevation (feet)
- 7,500
- 7,000
- 6,500
- 6,000
- 5,500
- 5,000
- 4,500

N

0   Kilometer   0.35

0   Mile

Sunrise Ranger Station

Sunrise Visitor Center

Emmons Vista

To White River Auto Camp

Sourdough Ridge Nature Trail

Sourdough Ridge Trail

YAKIMA PARK

To Forest Lake

Huckleberry Creek Trail

Frozen Lake

To Mount Fremont Lookout

Mount Fremont Trail

Wonderland Trail

To Berkeley Park

Burroughs Mountain Trail

First Burroughs Mountain

To Glacier Basin & White River Auto Camp

MOUNT RAINIER NATIONAL PARK

Sunrise Rim Trail

Shadow Lake

Sunrise Camp

and then it travels gradually uphill all the way to the Sunrise Complex parking lot.

Miles and Directions

0.0 Start from the Sunrise parking lot, and follow the paved path to the right (east) of the restrooms, heading north. Don't let the road heading off to the left (west) tempt you; stay on the main trail, heading north past the informative display.

0.1 The Sourdough Ridge Nature Trail forks; stay to the left (northwest) toward Frozen Lake and Mount Fremont.

0.3 Reach the top of Sourdough Ridge and the junction with the Sourdough Ridge Trail. Take a left (west) onto the trail.

0.6 Bypass the steep Huckleberry Creek Trail on your right (north).

1.4 Just beyond Frozen Lake, come to the junction of five trails. Take the Burroughs Mountain Trail, heading southwest.

2.4 After going over the First Burroughs Mountain, you reach the junction with the southern section of the Sunrise Loop. At the junction take a left (east) toward Sunrise Camp along the southern Burroughs Mountain Trail toward Sunrise.

3.4 At the junction with the Sunrise Campground Trail, continue east, ignoring the administrative road on your left.

3.6 Just beyond Sunrise Camp, come to Shadow Lake.

4.4 Beyond Shadow Lake, reach another trail junction. This time, the Wonderland Trail is splitting off to your right (south). Continue east toward Sunrise.

4.9 At the intersection with the Silver Forest Trail, bear left (north) toward the Sunrise parking lot, and arrive at your car promptly.

25 Sourdough Ridge Nature Trail

This one-hour stroll up to and along Sourdough Ridge offers panoramic views and fantastic subalpine wildflowers.

Start: Sunrise Complex
Distance: 1.3-mile lollipop
Hiking time: 1 hour
Trail surface: Well-maintained; dirt trail and subalpine meadow
Elevation gain: Minimal
Best season: Mid-July through Sept
Nearest town: Greenwater

Fees and permits: Vehicle or individual entry fee (7 days); annual entry available; timed entry applies
Trail contacts: White River Wilderness Information Center, (360) 569-6670; Sunrise Visitor Center, (360) 663-2425

Finding the trailhead: From the White River Entrance Station, drive 13.8 miles west on the White River Road to the Sunrise Complex parking lot. Park and walk to the trailhead on the northwestern end of the lot, to the right of the restrooms. **GPS:** N46 54.948' / W121 38.623'

The Hike

For many years, the park maintained this short lollipop as an interpretive nature trail complete with thirteen informative stations. In 2012, the stations were pulled from the earth, but the trail remains worthwhile for its spectacular views and abundant subalpine flora. It also serves as the main trail access point for the network of trails in the Sunrise area.

Go to the northwestern part of the parking lot. Follow the wide trail that runs north beyond the restrooms. A map and display on the left (west) delineate trails in the Sunrise area, including elevation charts and short descriptions.

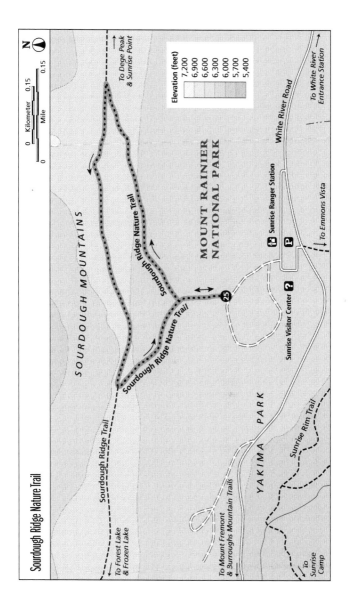

Sourdough Ridge Nature Trail

N

0   Kilometer   0.15
0   Mile   0.15

Elevation (feet)
7,200
6,900
6,600
6,300
6,000
5,700
5,400

SOURDOUGH MOUNTAINS

Sourdough Ridge Trail

To Dege Peak
& Sunrise Point

Sourdough Ridge Nature Trail

Sourdough Ridge Nature Trail

25

MOUNT RAINIER
NATIONAL PARK

Sunrise Ranger Station

P

Sunrise Visitor Center   ?

White River Road

To White River
Entrance Station

To Emmons Vista

To Forest Lake
& Frozen Lake

YAKIMA
PARK

To Mount Fremont
& Burroughs Mountain Trails

Sunrise Rim Trail

To
Sunrise
Camp

Continue north on this trail another 0.1 mile until it forks. Follow the sign pointing right (east) toward Sourdough Ridge. Take your time in this subalpine park. Turn around; you have a fantastic view of the grandeur of Mount Rainier. All around you, the delicate meadow bursts with lupine, American bistort, paintbrush, pasqueflower, subalpine daisy, fanleaf cinquefoil, aster, and spreading phlox.

At the top of the ridge, 0.5 mile into your hike, the path forks again. Take the left (west) fork. For the next 0.5 mile, you walk along the top of Sourdough Ridge with views off both sides of the ridge. On a clear day you can see Mount Baker, Mount Adams, and Glacier Peak.

At the next trail junction, turn left (south). The Sunrise Complex comes into sight as the lollipop reaches its stem in just over 0.1 mile. Follow the wide main trail another 0.2 mile to its inception.

Miles and Directions

0.0   Head north along the main hiking trail, which starts to the right (east) of the restrooms at the Sunrise Complex and ascends to Sourdough Ridge. A sign gives information about the trails in the Sunrise area.

0.2   The trail forks, head right (east).

0.5   The trail intersects with Sourdough Ridge Trail, turn left (west) and walk along the top of the ridge.

1.0   The Sourdough Ridge Trail intersects with the main trail to Sunrise, take a hard left (southeast) heading downhill toward the Sunrise Complex.

1.1   You reach the location where the trail originally forked, head due south to Sunrise.

1.3   Arrive back at the trailhead.

26 Dege Peak

A short climb to the top of Dege Peak affords views of Mount Rainier, the North Cascades, Mount Adams, Mount Baker, and Sunrise Lake.

Start: Sunrise Point
Distance: 2.8 miles out and back
Hiking time: 1.5-2 hours
Trail surface: Well-maintained; subalpine meadow and rocky alpine terrain
Elevation gain: 928 feet
Best season: Mid-July through Sept

Nearest town: Greenwater
Fees and permits: Vehicle or individual entry fee (7 days); annual entry available; timed entry applies
Trail contacts: White River Wilderness Information Center, (360) 569-6670; Sunrise Visitor Center, (360) 663-2425

Finding the trailhead: From the White River Ranger Station, continue 11 miles on White River Road to well-marked Sunrise Point. **GPS:** N46 55.042' / W121 35.373'

The Hike

Although this hike is only 2.8 miles long, you climb uphill for the entire 1.4-mile trip to Dege Peak. Make sure to bring plenty of water, and pace yourself throughout the climb. From the top of Dege Peak, jaw-dropping scenery surrounds you in every direction.

The Sourdough Ridge Trail begins from the west end of the parking lot; head west. Subalpine wildflowers, such as lupine and magenta paintbrush, often line the trail in mid-summer, and trees provide much-needed shade on a hot day.

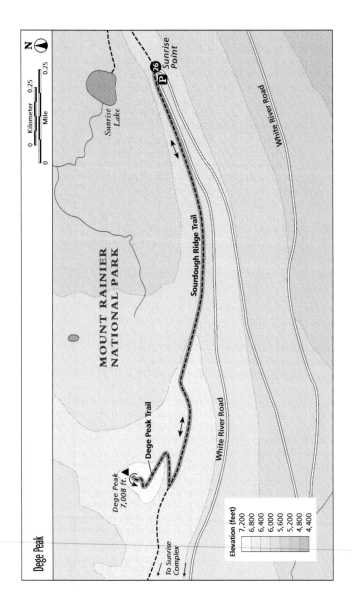

Dege Peak

MOUNT RAINIER NATIONAL PARK

Dege Peak
7,008 ft.

Dege Peak Trail

To Sunrise Complex

Sourdough Ridge Trail

White River Road

White River Road

Sunrise Lake

Sunrise Point

P 26

N

0   Kilometer   0.25
0   Mile   0.25

Elevation (feet)
7,200
6,800
6,400
6,000
5,600
5,200
4,800
4,400

Marcus Peak rises on the right (north), and when you have gained enough elevation, Mount Rainier comes into view to the west.

After hiking 1.1 miles, you come to the junction with the Dege Peak Trail. Turn right (northeast) on this trail. It is only 0.3 mile to the summit from this point, but the trail follows steep switchbacks all the way to the top. At the top of Dege Peak you have entered the alpine zone. The peak consists of rock; little vegetation grows on the rocky surface. You can see two dormant volcanoes, Mount Baker and Mount Adams, and enjoy an impressive view of majestic Mount Rainier.

When you decide to head back, it is all downhill! Relish the view of Clover and Sunrise Lakes as you descend the peak. Sunrise Lake is closest to Sunrise Point, where you began your hike; Clover Lake is farther north, near Marcus Peak.

Miles and Directions

0.0   Start heading west on the Sourdough Ridge Trail from the west end of the Sunrise Point parking lot.

1.1   At the junction with the Dege Peak Trail, turn right (northeast) and begin the steep climb to Dege Peak.

1.4   Reach Dege Peak summit. Enjoy the view and then begin your descent.

2.8   Arrive back at the trailhead.

27 Spray Falls

This hike travels over several small ridges through beautiful forest to striking Spray Falls, which provides tired hikers with a nice misting on hot summer days.

Start: Mowich Lake
Distance: 4.0 miles out and back
Hiking time: 1.5–2.5 hours
Trail surface: Well-maintained; forest floor
Elevation gain: Minimal
Best season: Early July through Sept

Nearest town: Wilkeson
Fees and permits: Vehicle or individual entry fee (7 days); annual entry available; no timed entry required
Trail contacts: Carbon River Ranger Station, (360) 829-9639

Finding the trailhead: From Wilkeson, drive 9 miles south on WA 165 until the road forks. Stay to the right (south) at this fork, the way to Mowich Lake. After 3.2 miles the road turns into a well-maintained dirt road, although it can be very slippery when muddy and dusty washboard when dry. Follow this road for another 8.8 miles to the Paul Peak Trailhead on the right (south) side of the road. You can pause here to pay the entrance fee at the fee station. Continue south and east 5.3 miles to Mowich Lake, a total of 26.3 miles from Wilkeson. The parking lot is fairly big, but on sunny weekends you might have to park along the road. **GPS:** N46 55.951' / W121 51.799'

The Hike

This hike has no significant elevation gain, but it trundles over rather steep hills all the way to Spray Falls. A trail construction crew named Spray Falls in 1883 because they felt that the cascading falls broke "into a mass of spray." The well-maintained, heavily used trail winds through beautiful forest. Expect to see many other park visitors; please reduce your impact by staying on the trail.

Head to the south end of Mowich Lake, past the restrooms and Mowich Lake Campground to the Wonderland Trail. Go south on the Wonderland Trail for a little over 0.2 mile to the junction with the Spray Park Trail. Go left (southeast) when the Spray Park Trail forks off from the Wonderland Trail. About a mile after the junction, a short spur trail from the junction leads to an overlook from Eagle Cliff, a total of 1.5 miles into your hike. You can see the North Mowich Glacier clearly from the lookout.

At 0.3 mile past the lookout, you will see the signs for Eagle's Roost Camp. Eagle's Roost Camp is less than 0.1 mile away from the Spray Park Trail. At the junction with Spray Falls Trail, 0.1 mile past Eagle's Roost Camp, turn right (southeast) toward the falls.

The falls drop roughly 300 feet. At the top of the falls, the water sprays off the mossy rocks, leaving the air misty and cool. Lewis's and yellow monkeyflowers line Spray Creek, adding to the beauty of this natural wonder.

Miles and Directions

0.0 Start at Mowich Lake. Head to the south end of the lake, past the restrooms and Mowich Lake Campground to the Wonderland Trail.

0.2 Arrive at the junction with the Spray Park Trail and go left (southeast) onto the trail.

1.5 A spur trail to the Eagle Cliff vista darts down the ridge to your right (west). Take this very short side trip to enjoy the best view on the hike.

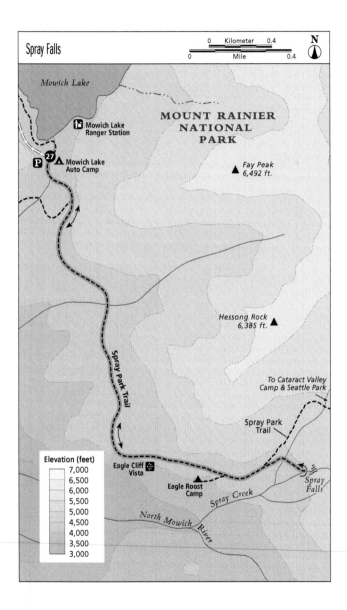

Spray Falls

0   Kilometer   0.4
0   Mile   0.4

N

Mowich Lake

Mowich Lake
Ranger Station

**MOUNT RAINIER
NATIONAL
PARK**

▲ *Fay Peak*
6,492 ft.

P ㉗ ▲ Mowich Lake
Auto Camp

Hessong Rock
6,385 ft. ▲

Spray Park Trail

*To Cataract Valley
Camp & Seattle Park*

Spray Park
Trail

Eagle Cliff
Vista

▲
Eagle Roost
Camp

Spray Creek

⚡ *Spray
Falls*

North Mowich River

Elevation (feet)

7,000
6,500
6,000
5,500
5,000
4,500
4,000
3,500
3,000

1.8	Reach a spur trail, which heads south to Eagle's Roost Camp. Stay to the left (east).
1.9	Reach the junction with Spray Falls Trail. Turn right.
2.0	Arrive at Spray Falls. Enjoy the falls before retracing your steps.
4.0	Arrive back at Mowich Lake.

28 Tolmie Peak

This very popular hike travels through forest and meadow to a fire lookout atop Tolmie Peak, which offers a spectacular view of the northwestern side of Mount Rainier. The trail also takes you by serene Eunice Lake, a lake surrounded by jutting peaks and subalpine forest.

Start: Mowich Lake
Distance: 6.4 miles out and back
Hiking time: 3–4.5 hours
Trail surface: Well-maintained; forest floor to rocky ridge trail
Elevation gain: 1,020 feet
Best season: Mid-July through Sept

Nearest town: Wilkeson
Fees and permits: Vehicle or individual entry fee (7 days); annual entry available; no timed entry required
Trail contacts: Carbon River Ranger Station, (360) 829-9639

Finding the trailhead: From Wilkeson drive 9 miles south on WA 165. Where Carbon River Road joins in, stay to the right on WA 165. The pavement ends 3.2 miles beyond the intersection. Drive along a dirt road for 8.8 miles to reach the park boundary; pause here to pay the entry fee at the fee station. Continue another 5.3 miles to Mowich Lake Campground, which has a small parking lot. Many trails originate here; the trail to Tolmie Peak (Wonderland Trail) will be to your immediate left, heading north along the west side of the lake. **GPS:** N46 55.982' / W121 51.791'

The Hike

The hike to Tolmie Peak is one of the most popular in the northwest region of Mount Rainier National Park for many reasons. Neither too long nor too rigorous, it provides the opportunity to explore subalpine forests and a serene lake as well as catch a breathtaking panorama of Mount Rainier.

Tolmie Peak and Tolmie Peak Trail are named for Dr. William Fraser Tolmie. This doctor, led by Nisqually headman Lahalet, was the first-recorded non–Native American to approach Mount Rainier. Unlike others to follow him, he wasn't focused on ascending to the summit, but rather just wanted to collect herbs for medicinal purposes and simply enjoy the captivating scenery. Records indicate that he ascended all the way to Hessong Rock.

From the Mowich Lake parking lot, go to the Wonderland Trail, which runs along the west side of Mowich Lake. There are several paths down to this trail, but the only trail that runs north–south along Mowich Lake is the Wonderland Trail. Head north on the Wonderland Trail. The trail hugs the west side of Mowich Lake for about 0.5 mile before leaving the lake and heading north. After reaching the top of a small hill on the north side of Mowich Lake, continue on flat terrain to the junction with the Tolmie Peak Trail. At the junction, the Wonderland Trail drops to the right (north) down through Ipsut Pass toward the Ipsut Creek Campground, and the Tolmie Peak Trail proceeds to the left (northwest). Take the Tolmie Peak Trail toward Eunice Lake and Tolmie Peak.

After turning, you immediately begin to descend steeply. At the bottom of this hill, the trail forks. The trail to the left is an unmaintained social trail created by those eager to see a small waterfall only a few paces off the beaten path. Stay to the right (north) to continue the journey to Eunice Lake and Tolmie Peak.

The trail begins a steep climb up switchbacks. As you crest the hill, a sign points the way to Tolmie Peak. Stay to the left (west) on the marked trail around the lake. As you approach Eunice Lake, you step into a field blanketed by avalanche lilies in mid-July or huckleberries in late summer. A series of jutting, rocky peaks top a vertical wall on the far side of the lake. If you look closely, you can see the lookout from the lakeside. Try to stay on the trail. The meadow is fragile, and off-trail hikers can cause lasting damage to its delicate vegetation. Eunice is a really pretty tarn, but your real prize awaits you: At the top of the ridge proudly sits the Tolmie Peak lookout. And the view of Eunice Lake and the surrounding area from atop the ridge beats the scene from its shore.

When the trail reaches the northwestern part of the lake, it begins to ascend by means of steady switchbacks to the top of the ridge. After you turn the corner on your last switch-back, you have reached the top of the ridge and are afforded an expansive view of rolling mountains to the north with their patchwork of clear-cuts. Better, though, is the view of Mount Rainier; if you manage to get a clear day, it is simply spectacular. To the south is one of the best panoramic views of Mount Rainier available in the park. Less than 0.25 mile beyond your final switchback towers the Tolmie Peak fire lookout and your destination. If open, climb to the deck of the lookout and examine the humble accommodations and some interesting informational displays.

The more adventurous can carefully follow the unmaintained trail along a ridge toward the true Tolmie Peak. The trail is not steep, but it is rocky and a bit tricky at points; a fall could be very serious. Tread carefully while you take in

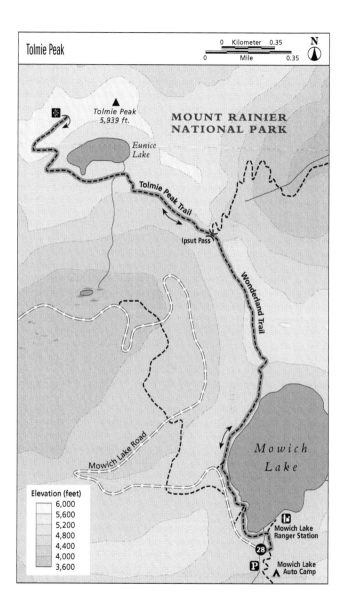

Tolmie Peak

| 0 | Kilometer | 0.35 |
| 0 | Mile | 0.35 |

N

Tolmie Peak
5,939 ft.

Eunice Lake

MOUNT RAINIER
NATIONAL PARK

Tolmie Peak Trail

Ipsut Pass

Wonderland Trail

Mowich Lake Road

Mowich Lake

Elevation (feet)
6,000
5,600
5,200
4,800
4,400
4,000
3,600

Mowich Lake
Ranger Station

28

P

Mowich Lake
Auto Camp

your surroundings, and then find your way back along the same path.

Miles and Directions

0.0 Start at the Mowich Lake parking lot. Find the Wonderland Trail, which runs along the west side of Mowich Lake. There are several paths down to this trail, but the only trail that runs north–south along Mowich Lake is the Wonderland Trail. Head north on the Wonderland Trail.

1.5 At the Tolmie Peak Trail junction, turn left (northwest).

2.4 Stay to the left (west) on the marked trail around Eunice Lake.

3.1 Reach the Tolmie Peak Lookout and the end of the maintained trail.

3.2 A steep and rocky unmaintained trail takes you to the top of Tolmie Peak. Carefully make your way back to the main trail, and then head back to the trailhead.

6.4 Arrive back at the parking lot.

29 Old Mine Trail

A casual walk along the permanently closed Carbon River Road leads to an extremely steep, but short ascent to the entrance to a decommissioned mine.

Start: Carbon River Entrance

Distance: 3.0 miles out and back

Hiking time: 1 hour

Trail surface: Well-maintained; dirt road, forest floor

Elevation gain: Minimal

Best season: May through Oct

Nearest town: Wilkeson

Fees and permits: Vehicle or individual entry fee (7 days); annual entry available; no timed entry required

Trail contacts: Carbon River Ranger Station, (360) 829-9639

Finding the trailhead: From Wilkeson drive 9 miles south on WA 165. Where Carbon River Road intersects with WA 165, stay to the left toward Carbon River Entrance. After 6 miles, you reach the Carbon River Ranger Station. You may stop to pay the entrance fee here, and travel another 2 miles to the entrance station and the trailhead. Park in one of the designated spots or along the road. **GPS:** N46 59.700' / W121 54.902'

The Hike

The closure of the Carbon River Road has significantly reduced the amount of traffic in the Carbon River Area. Trails like Chenuis Falls and Green Lake, which once provided day hikers with easy treks in the woods and lovely destinations, have become unworkable for many hikers with the added miles to reach what once was a drive-to trailhead.

Old Mine Trail

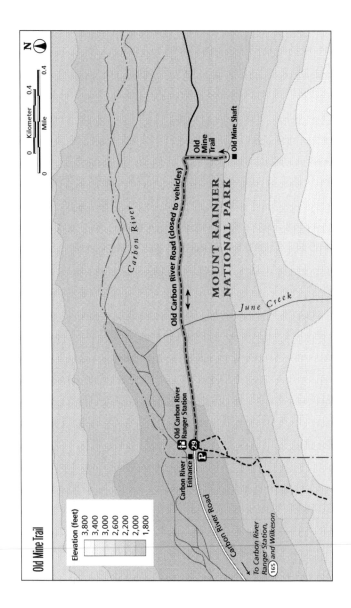

Elevation (feet)
- 3,800
- 3,400
- 3,000
- 2,600
- 2,200
- 2,000
- 1,800

To Carbon River
Ranger Station,
and Wilkeson
165

Carbon River Road

Carbon River
Entrance

Old Carbon River
Ranger Station

Old Carbon River Road (closed to vehicles)

Carbon River

June Creek

MOUNT RAINIER
NATIONAL PARK

Old
Mine
Trail

Old Mine Shaft

Kilometer
0   0.4

Mile
0   0.4

N

Few options remain for the casual day hiker. The Old Mine Trail is one of those options.

The first 1.2 miles of "trail" follows the Carbon River Road. As you would expect, the flat grade and nonexistent trail hazards make this portion of the hike fast going. The Carbon River, though largely obscured by the massive Douglas firs and other old growth, parallels the road to the left (north). If you listen, you will hear the occasional crash of glacial debris tumbling down its silt-ridden waters.

Sooner than you would expect, a small parking area comes into view on the right (south), along with the trailhead sign directing you to the "Old Mine," formerly the Washington Mining and Milling Company Trailhead.

Head south on this trail, into the calm of the temperate rain forest. The portion of trail to the mine shaft is short but remarkably steep. Winded at the top, you can peer into the mine shaft, but boards prevent you from entering beyond a few feet. Bat habitat study and preservation is a plan for this area. When done, just retrace your steps.

Miles and Directions

0.0 The hike begins at the Carbon River Entrance. Head east along the Carbon River Road where the closure begins.

1.2 After just over a mile of relatively flat hiking on wide road, you come to an area once used for trailhead parking and a signpost, marking the trailhead to the "Old Mine" on your right (south).

1.5 A very steep ascent has brought you to your destination: the defunct old mine shaft now used as bat habitat. At this point, you can turn and head back the way you came.

3.0 Arrive back at the entrance station.

30 Carbon River Rainforest Trail

A very short and flat loop through temperate rain forest with educational signs posted throughout, this informative nature walk is perfect for families with small children and adults looking for a peaceful stroll just outside the park.

Start: Carbon River Entrance
Distance: 0.3-mile loop
Hiking time: 20–30 minutes
Trail surface: Well-maintained; forest floor and boardwalk
Elevation gain: Minimal
Best season: May through Oct

Nearest town: Wilkeson
Fees and permits: Vehicle or individual entry fee (7 days); annual entry available; no timed entry required
Trail contacts: Carbon River Ranger Station, (360) 829-9639

Finding the trailhead: From Wilkeson drive 9 miles south on WA 165. Where Carbon River Road intersects with WA 165, stay to the left toward Carbon River Entrance. After 6 miles, you reach the Carbon River Ranger Station. You may stop to pay the entrance fee here, and travel another 2 miles to the entrance station and the trailhead. Park in one of the designated spots or along the road. **GPS:** N46 59.693' / W121 54.917'

The Hike

This short nature walk has become a more popular option in the Carbon River area since the permanent closure of the Carbon River Road rendered other hikes unattainable for many day hikers. This educational nature walk is perfect for children and people of limited abilities, though it would not quite qualify as wheelchair accessible.

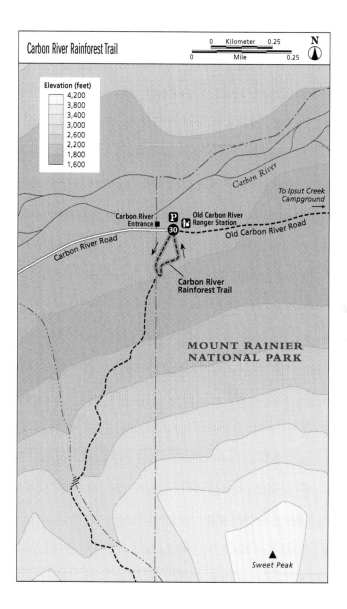

Carbon River Rainforest Trail

0 Kilometer 0.25
0 Mile 0.25

N

Elevation (feet)
4,200
3,800
3,400
3,000
2,600
2,200
1,800
1,600

Carbon River

To Ipsut Creek
Campground →

Carbon River
Entrance ■

Old Carbon River
Ranger Station

Old Carbon River Road

Carbon River Road

Carbon River
Rainforest Trail

MOUNT RAINIER
NATIONAL PARK

Sweet Peak

There is little need for direction along this hike. It is well-marked and well-maintained. A boardwalk has been placed on the forest floor to protect hikers from the mud and remediate the erosive effects of tromping boots on the forest. Signs posted throughout discuss the ecosystem of a temperate rainforest, including the weather, the canopy, and the fauna in its various sections. A curious child will absorb the information like a sponge and enjoy the hands-on learning opportunity.

About halfway through the hike, you come to the junction with the West Boundary Trail on your right (south). Stay to the left and complete the loop back to the Carbon River Entrance.

Miles and Directions

0.0 Well-marked by large signs, the trail heads south across from the old site of the Carbon River Ranger Station.

0.1 The West Boundary Trail heads off up the hill to the right (south).

0.3 The loop is complete; arrive back at the trailhead.

Meet Your Guides

We grew up climbing mountains together. The great expanse of our home state, Montana, sparked a reverence of the wilderness and a zest for adventure in both of us. Mount Rainier, or Tahoma, inspired a sense of awe and admiration from our first introduction to its slopes in the summer of 1998, when we hiked every foot of trail as teenagers. We have been hooked ever since.

We both came to Portland after high school, but on different journeys. Mary's path took her to pursue justice through civil rights law and Heidi's path to heal as a physician. At the time we initially wrote the book, we were in college in Portland—Mary at Reed and Heidi at Lewis and Clark College. We have now completed five revisions of the book over the course of 25 years whilst growing cherished families and passionate careers.

Just as we have grown and changed, the park has shifted over the years: impressive visitor facilities have been built, fees have increased, the rules and regulations have been revised, and nature has reshaped the topography. The extreme increase in popularity and exposure has been the most notable change in the last few years. Lines that once caused frustration are now interminable. You must plan ahead. May the information and guidance in this book allow you to have the best-laid plans and most ideal itinerary for your next adventure on our home away from home.

For us, the mountain's beauty and enchantment remain a constant source of joy and a regular test of resilience. We hope to prepare you for your adventure so you may fall in love with this place like we have.

THE TEN ESSENTIALS OF HIKING

American Hiking Society

Whether you plan to be gone for a couple of hours or several months, make sure to pack these items. Become familiar with these items and know how to use them.

Find other helpful resources at AmericanHiking.org/hiking-resources

1. **Appropriate Footwear**

2. **Navigation**

3. **Water** (and a way to purify it)

4. **Food**

5. **Rain Gear & Dry-Fast Layers**

6. **Safety Items** (light, fire, and a whistle)

7. **First Aid Kit**

8. **Knife or Multi-Tool**

9. **Sun Protection**

10. **Shelter**